PTION DEPARTMENT

SERENDIPITY
PARTIES

DISCARD

SERENDIPITY PARTIES

PLEASANTLY UNEXPECTED
IDEAS FOR ENTERTAINING

STEPHEN BRUCE

WITH SARAH KEY
PHOTOS BY LIZ STEGER

ILLUSTRATIONS BY SEYMOUR CHWAST

UNIVERSE

TABLE OF CONTENTS

INTRODUCTION

When you leave the hustle and bustle of 60th Street for Serendipity, you feel like Alice entering Wonderland. It's not just a tea party going on inside, but a mad, mad adventure with fantasy décor, ice cream treats galore, and an eccentric general store to boot. The story of Serendipity begins in 1954 when I teamed up with Calvin Holt and Patch Carradine. We first opened the restaurant in a low-ceilinged basement on 58th Street—just a natural extension of the parties we'd been throwing in our equally tiny cold-water flat. We catered to our pals: actors, designers, and other artistic types trying to make it in the Big Apple. Serendipity became the place to throw a party. Here, Victoriana meets mod, and we serve Aunt Buba's Sand Tarts as well as Foot-long Hot Dogs. It's impossible not to feel festive as you sip our over-the-top Frrrozen Hot Chocolate or down a Forbidden Broadway Sundae. On our Tiffany lamp-lit journey, we've learned a thing or two about how to give a party. Here we share with you those ideas and tips.

While the first rule for parties is "plan, plan, plan," it is often the unexpected, serendipitous moments that will be remembered. Take, for instance, my fateful first real encounter with Andy Warhol. Never could I have expected that the great artist would have dropped in to Serendipity and spent the afternoon sketching away. But that is just what happened. To create an atmosphere that lends itself to these special happenings—this is our party philosophy. Make sure that you leave room within the planning for such odd surprises.

Good parties beget good friends, and in 1954 we made two, the now-legendary graphic designers Seymour Chwast and Milton Glaser, who had just started Push Pin Studios and who created our 3 Princes logo. Milton went on to design the iconic "I♥NY," and Seymour executed some of the most eye-popping posters of the psychedelic era. Almost ten years ago, we were honored to have Seymour create our cool Ice Queen and red-hot Devil, the two beloved characters who cavort at the start of each chapter in this book.

One never knows what will start your party popping. Andy loved the sweet comfort of Miss Essie Vaughn's Lemon Ice Box Pie, but maybe it was our antique espresso machine that fueled his imagination too. A serendipitous convergence of drink and décor! This espresso machine is just one of hundreds of unique *objets* in the restaurant that serve as attractive conversation pieces. To find your own, start as we did in flea markets, garage sales, and antique stores. You can dress up your offerings without spending a fortune. Whatever food or drink you do serve, make sure it is fresh and fun. The savory dishes presented here make delicious appetizers and finger food. We think it's best to keep party food light and sweet. You want guests bubbling over with excitement, not dozing off in a postprandial slumber.

From the beginning, we called Serendipity 3 a "general store," but it has never been your typical market with bread and milk. Instead we started stocking up on things that might come in handy if you were going to the Mad Hatter's tea party! Our boutique has a sense of humor. Where else can Shirley Temple dishware, marabou-trimmed hats, Victorian soap dishes, voodoo kits, Buck Rogers stationery, and Warhol silkscreened cats all frolic together? Having quirky items like these around helps give a party just the right touches. Here we give you loads of ideas for creating your own unusual party items—whether it's making your own Ouija board or putting together a Sailor's Valentine out of seashells.

Whatever celebration you have planned, open your mind up to the endless possibilities of unexpected pleasures, and you will bump into a good time no matter what direction you take.

—*Stephen Bruce*

CHAPTER ONE

VALENTINE'S DAY SERENDIPITY'S WAY:

SEASHELL CARDS AND HOT CHOCOLATE

So you want unconventional? How about getting married on Valentine's Day with your feet in a tub of Frrrozen Hot Chocolate and wearing a chocolate satin Vera Wang wedding dress and a Harry Winston chocolate diamond? Then the groom drinks a cocoa toast from your designer shoes, which have been filled with liquid chocolate. It's been done, but only at Serendipity.

Valentine's Day is all about seduction, so take your time and plan ahead. If you don't have a vat of chocolate lying around, set the mood by booking a private room in a great restaurant. Decorate the table with pink candles, make sure the light is low, and arrange for special dishes with the chef. Write the menu in an ornate script on an antique valentine and place one on each plate. If you don't have a lot of money to spend, find a local restaurant with reasonable prices or make dinner at home. The key is to add a few personal touches so the affair feels both intimate and elegant. Style the evening to suit the specific taste of your beloved, whether he or she is into chocolate or bling or punk rock.

Sometimes it's the height of romance simply to hold hands—even for the rich and famous. When Nicole Kidman and her country-singer beau Keith Urban dined at Serendipity, they entwined hands throughout the meal, which made chowing down burgers with blue cheese a charmingly romantic challenge. But they prevailed, hampered by neither her fitted white blouse nor his clingy blue jeans. Oh, the things we do for love.

PARTY MENU

CHUNKS OF LOBSTER WITH
MELTED BUTTER FOR DIPPING

OYSTERS ON THE HALF SHELL

ARTICHOKES OR ASPARAGUS
WITH HOLLANDAISE

BLUSHING FONDUE
(page 17)
OR
BI-SENSUAL CHOCOLATE FONDUE
(page 16)

MILE-HIGH RASPBERRY PIE
(page 18)

OLD-FASHIONED DIVINITY WITH
A MINTY TWIST
(page 19)

FROZEN GRAPES

WARHOL'S WHIMSY: MY FUNNY VALENTINE

One afternoon in 1954, Andy Warhol came into Serendipity as he often did for a cappuccino and dessert. At the time, he was producing artwork for shoe ads and for a glamour magazine. By late afternoon, work was usually over, drowned in multiple-martini lunches. On this particular day, he seemed content to fill his brand-new sketch pad with what he was happened to be feeling—and the pages danced with hearts, ranging in size from pupil-small to tie-knot big, making words superfluous. With just a few distinct lines, he captured my sloping forehead, snub nose, curls pressed tight to the head, closed mouth, and striped dandy shirt. Over the next few hours, he proceeded to unfurl a bouquet of feelings in a series of twenty-four drawings he called "Play Book of you S. Bruce from 2:30–4:00." Treasure all your funny valentines.

SAILORS' VALENTINES

Serendipity has always had a passion for antiques. Starting out, we furnished the restaurant and stocked the general store with treasures and trinkets found on weekend antiquing raids in upstate New York. When Valentine's Day would come around, the curios and collectibles for sale at Serendipity took on a noticeably romantic blush.

One particularly eccentric antique that we fell in love with is called the sailor's valentine. At the height of the Victorian age, the Caribbean island of Barbados was a bustling port of call for seafarers. Craftsmen on the island would gather tiny, brilliantly colored shells that littered the white sand beaches to create stunningly intricate mosaics within octagonal boxes, often inscribed with love notes. These sailors' valentines quickly became a favorite souvenir to send back to sweethearts. Rare and highly prized today, these extraordinary valentines evoke a lost age of ardent devotion and high seas adventure. They've inspired us to create our own valentine in the same tradition. It's surprisingly easy to replicate the idea at home. Here's how:

1. Find a shallow round gift box with a lid. Line the inside with rosy pink paper. Cover the outside of the box with colored paper and decorative ribbon.

2. Choose a variety of very small, colorful seashells. Craft stores and online companies sell varied assortments. Select a larger, dramatic shell, such as the cardium cardissa heart used below. Arrange shells around the center to create neat rows, spirals, or rings. Using a hot glue gun, neutral-pH craft glue, or airplane glue, carefully glue the shells into place. Attach the lid to the valentine with a ribbon or small hinge.

LANGUAGE
OF FLOWERS

Serendipity's upstairs Victorian parlor with its pastel putti on the walls, marble-top tables, and mirrored butterflies suggests a bygone era, a lost language of love. When a bouquet of flowers was assembled in the mid-1800s, it carried a specific message. A letter or card was unnecessary as the flowers and foliage had assigned meanings. Feelings and sentiments that were considered inappropriate to speak out loud could be expressed more subtly this way. For example, a bridal bouquet consisting of blue violets and forget-me-knots surrounded by ivy is a sign of faithfulness and enduring love in marriage. To fend off a potential suitor with an offer of friendship, you might send orange blossoms and acacia leaves to declare your chastity. And at the end of a party, you might give your secret admirer a bouquet like the one shown here (begonias, maidenhair fern, and chrysanthemums) to announce, "I know your secret."

PLAYING FOR LOVE

1. "Where Is My Love," Cat Power
2. "Where Does the Good Go,"
   Tegan and Sara
3. "A Little Bit Me, A Little Bit You,"
   The Monkees
4. "Photobooth," Death Cab for Cutie
5. "The Celibate Life," The Shins
6. "My Heart Stood Still," Joe Williams
   and George Shearing
7. "Tear Your Love Apart," Gomez
8. "Crazy Little Thing Called Love,"
   Queen
9. "Hate," Cat Power
10. "Hello, I Love You," The Doors
11. "You Wouldn't Like Me,"
    Tegan and Sara
12. "Don't Look Back," Télépopmusik
13. "Little Lover," AC/DC
14. "The Mating Game," Bitter:Sweet
15. "Blood Is Love," Queens of the
    Stone Age
16. "Fools in Love," Inara George
17. "What You Meant," Franz Ferdinand

Since ancient Greek and Roman times, many foods have had a reputation for inspiring love. Some are said to increase male potency, others help boost fertility, while still others were chosen for their resemblance to parts of the human body.

ALMOND: Symbol of fertility. Marzipan is sometimes made in erotic shapes.

ANISEED: Greeks and Romans believed that anise seeds increase desire. Acts as a natural breath freshener.

ARUGULA: Also known as "rocket." Considered an aphrodisiac since the first century AD. Delicious in salads.

ASPARAGUS: Steam or lightly boil this vegetable and serve by hand.

AVOCADO: Slice and serve with a drizzle of balsamic vinegar and fresh ground pepper.

BASIL: Thought to boost fertility. Serve as part of a salad or as a garnish.

CHOCOLATE: Contains chemicals believed to effect neurotransmitters in the brain. Pair with a good red wine.

FIG: Eat ripe figs with your fingers. Sprinkle with balsamic vinegar, wrap in prosciutto, or serve with a little honey and ricotta cheese.

GINGER: Stimulates circulation. Grate into a stir-fry or make a tea infusion.

NUTMEG: Can be hallucinogenic if taken in quantity. Add to pancake batter or sprinkle on fruit salad.

OYSTERS: According to Roman literature dating from the second century AD, women turned wild after eating oysters and drinking wine.

PINE NUTS: Not nuts at all but rather seeds, these are rich in zinc, an important mineral for men.

RASPBERRIES AND STRAWBERRIES: The perfect fruit for hand-feeding your lover that is often mentioned in erotic literature.

SWEET HEART HISTORY

How do you say "I love you" in the sweetest way possible? For more than a century, the makers of NECCO Sweethearts Conversation Hearts have been saying "Kiss Me," "Sweet Talk," and "Be Mine." Certain mottoes on the candy hearts come and go, but some may be gone for good. Two that have been deemed outdated by NECCO are the funky "Dig Me" and the cheerful "You Are Gay."

Messages from more recent years include "Fit for Love," "Class Act," "ILU," "Whiz Kid," "Sweet Home," "Pen Pal," "Home Sick," "Be My Hero," "Heart of Gold," "School Mate," "Call Home," and "All-Star."

If you'd like to bring back some of the old sayings or devise new phrases, you can place a custom order—the only catch is that you have to buy a full production run of about 1.7 million candies. That's a lot of sweet hearts to handle.

SHIPWRECKED ON THE ISLE OF LOVE

We often forget that we are on an island in Manhattan, and even more so at Serendipity, where we are moored in a whimsical fantasy where the sweetest dreams tend to come true. Getting shipwrecked can be fun—and romantic—assuming you've got the right provisions for a party. Here are a few ideas:

INVITATIONS: Begin with "Get Shipwrecked on My Deserted Island" or "I Want You on My Deserted Island." This is an opportunity to blend nautical and Valentine's Day themes. The invitation can feature a sailor's knot in the shape of two hearts tied together.

COSTUME IDEA: Dress as your favorite *Gilligan's Island* character.

GAME: Put a sticker on everyone's back with a character from *Gilligan's Island*. Guests have to figure out who they are based on how others respond to them. No direct questions allowed.

ATMOSPHERE: In the background, play old episodes of *Gilligan's Island* on television.

GAME: The leader announces a theme (e.g., food, people, books, celebrities), and everyone takes turns saying what they would bring if they were shipwrecked on an island.

DRINKS: Make a large bowl of punch and give your guests hollowed coconut shells or tiki-themed cocktail glasses garnished with umbrellas.

BI-SENSUAL
CHOCOLATE FONDUE

12 ounces good-quality milk or dark chocolate

1 cup heavy cream

2 tablespoons brandy or rum (optional)

Fruit (whole strawberries, mandarin orange sections, banana slices, dried apricots)

Marshmallows

Cookies (Viennese fingers or ladyfingers)

Break the chocolate into 1-inch pieces and place in a fondue pot. Add the cream and heat slowly, stirring constantly, until the chocolate melts. If no fondue pot is available, melt the chocolate in a double boiler over simmering water, adding the cream in the same manner. Stir in the brandy or rum, if using.

Place the fondue pot (or the chocolate transferred from the double boiler to a heatproof pot or bowl) over a burner at the table, and serve with the fruit, marshmallows, and/or cookies for dipping.

Makes 6 to 8 servings

BLUSHING FONDUE

2 cups strawberries,
stems and hulls removed,
thawed if frozen

12 ounces white chocolate

1/2 cup heavy cream

Puree the strawberries in a food processor or blender. Strain out the seeds through a fine sieve. Break the chocolate into 1-inch pieces and place in a fondue pot. Add the cream and heat slowly, stirring constantly, until the chocolate melts. If no fondue pot is available, melt the chocolate in a double boiler over simmering water, adding the cream in the same manner. Add the strawberry puree and stir well.

Place the fondue pot (or the chocolate transferred from the double boiler to a heatproof pot or bowl) over a burner at the table and serve as above with the fruit, marshmallows, and/or cookies for dipping.

VARIATION: For a simpler version, omit the strawberries and add a few drops of red food coloring to the melted chocolate. It is easier to control the color this way, and the color is slightly prettier than that of the strawberries (though not as tasty).

Makes 6 to 8 servings

MILE-HIGH RASPBERRY PIE

2 (10-ounce) packages frozen raspberries

2 envelopes unflavored gelatin

1 1/4 cups sugar

4 egg whites

1 cup heavy cream

1 (10-inch) pie shell, baked

Shredded sweetened coconut

Thaw the raspberries and drain the juice into a measuring cup. Add cold water, if necessary, to make 1 cup of liquid. Soften the gelatin in the raspberry liquid.

Combine 1 cup of the sugar and 3/4 cup of water in a saucepan. Stir over low heat until the sugar dissolves. Cook until the temperature reaches 235 degrees F on a candy thermometer, or until a spoonful of syrup dropped in ice water will make a soft, sticky ball that will flatten when taken out of the water.

While cooking, use a whisk or an electric mixer to beat the egg whites until soft peaks form.

Add the gelatin mixture to the syrup and stir to dissolve. Slowly pour the syrup mixture over the beaten egg whites while beating rapidly. Continue beating until the mixture forms stiff peaks when the beater is raised.

In a separate bowl, whip the cream with the remaining 1/4 cup of sugar.

Fold the whipped cream into the egg white mixture. Fold in the drained raspberries. Spoon into the pie shell. Decorate with the shredded coconut. Chill for several hours or until set.

Makes one 10-inch pie, about 10 servings

OLD-FASHIONED DIVINITY WITH A MINTY TWIST

2 1/2 cups sugar

1/2 cup light corn syrup

1/4 teaspoon salt

2 egg whites

1 teaspoon vanilla extract

1/8 teaspoon mint extract (optional)

1 bunch mint leaves

Combine the sugar, corn syrup, and 1/2 cup of water in a medium-size saucepan. Cook until the mixture reaches the soft ball stage (234 to 242 degrees F on a candy thermometer). When a small spoonful of the liquid is dropped in ice water, it will make a pliable, sticky ball that flattens when removed from the water. Be careful not to overheat, as it will become too hard to work with.

In the bowl of an electric mixer, beat the salt and egg whites on high speed until stiff peaks form but before the mixture becomes dry. Reduce to medium speed and pour the syrup mixture into the egg whites in a steady stream. Beat the mixture until thick. Fold in the vanilla and the mint extract (if using).

Drop the mixture onto wax paper by teaspoonfuls and let cool. While cooling, gently press a whole mint leaf on top of each piece of divinity.

NOTE: This mixture, without the mint leaves, may also be used as cake icing. As such it also works well with the Star-for-a-Day Chocolate Cakes (page 44).

Makes about 3½ dozen

CHAPTER TWO

ACADEMY AWARDS GLAMOUR AT HOME:

RED CARPET LIVING ROOM

A t Serendipity we're all about style, and the night of the Academy Awards is the perfect time to show off your own sense of style with a dose of glamour. We first opened Serendipity on a shoestring, and yet we managed to throw parties that were perceived as lavish. Pulling off the perceived part is the trick. Even without much money, anyone can add touches of color, creativity, and elegance to liven up any space. Hollywood, after all, is about illusion and make-believe, so Oscar night is your opportunity to be a magician. Serve "caviar" and if it's really trout eggs, that is your secret. As long as you say it's caviar and it's your party, it is.

A party is also about creating a buzz, and that's why gossip columnists are so important. At Serendipity, some of our best friends are gossip columnists. Doris Lilly, the columnist who preceded Liz Smith at the *New York Post*, used to live around the corner from Serendipity and was a frequent customer. When she sold the rights to her book *How to Marry a Millionaire* for a lot of money, she came to the restaurant to celebrate. Take a page from the gossip columnists' manual and drum up excitement well before your Oscar night party. Spread a rumor that a big-name celebrity will make an appearance, but don't disappoint your guests. Make sure that the star shows up . . . or at least a celebrity look-alike!

PARTY MENU

CRUDITÉS WITH DIP

CAVIAR WITH BUCKWHEAT
BLINI (page 29)

LOBSTER SALAD

RED CARPET GELATIN WITH
BALSAMIC BERRIES (page 30)

TSARINA CHAMPAGNE
COCKTAIL (page 31)

CAPPUCCINO

ADMIT ONE TO A PRIVATE SCREENING

To create special movie-themed invitations, look for postcards decorated with classic movie posters. Then write your own customized message to paste on the address side of the cards. It's simple: Use a basic word processing program to make a text box to fit the postcards (most measure 4.25 x 6 inches). For a personal touch, leave space for handwriting the particulars or to include a special message. Using a glue stick or double-sided tape, affix your invitation to the back of the postcard, and carefully trim any overhang. If you plan to have an Oscar pool at your party (page 28), your guests can use these invitations as their entrance tickets.

You can adapt this invitation to your particular taste in movies—from 1930s MGM musicals to film noir to B-movies. You can even design the invitations to look like old-fashioned movie tickets, with ADMIT ONE stamped in bold across the top. Embellish the invitations with a famous line of dialogue to set the tone. Here are some of our favorites:

✳ "Fasten your seatbelts. It's going to be a bumpy night." *All About Eve*

✳ "All right, Mr. DeMille, I'm ready for my close-up." *Sunset Boulevard*

✳ "That's no moon." *Star Wars*

✳ "You mustn't give your heart to a wild thing." *Breakfast at Tiffany's*

✳ "Oh my God, the Bend and Snap—works every time!" *Legally Blonde*

A GRAND ENTRANCE

Arrange for your guests to enter your home in glam style by lifting up your everyday runner and laying down a red carpet. For less than ten dollars, you can find a fifteen-foot movie night red runner. Order one online or go to your local fabric store and request a piece of faux velvet cut to fit your entry hall. Secure the fabric with strong double-sided tape. Buy several disposable cameras and have them handy. As each guest arrives, the other guests can play "paparazzi" and snap photos of the new guests coming down the red carpet. For your red-carpet fete, assign one or more guests (with a good sense of humor) to be the party's Cindy Adams or Army Archerd and report on what they're seeing. Instead of watching the commercials on your TV, you can listen to the "professionals" gossip. Give your "reporters" a microphone, so they can interview the stars and ask them outrageous personal questions.

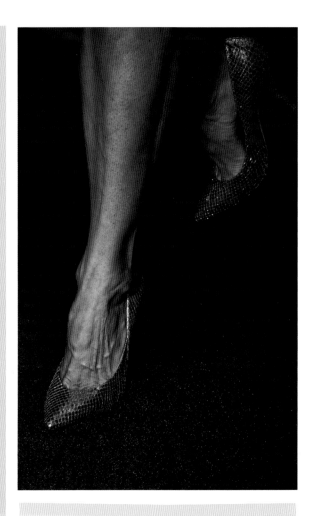

REMEMBER MY NAME

To dress up the dinner table, cut red felt circles in a variety of sizes or large silver paper stars to make your own Hollywood Walk of Fame runner with each guest's name on a star in silver or gold marker. Or write your guests' names on place cards using glittery red nail polish and tie a red or silver ribbon through them. Decorate the table with miniature disco balls and tie a silver ribbon around each napkin.

THE PRE-PARTY

For the movie stars who actually attend the Oscars, the fun starts way before they show up to take their seats at the award show. Shopping for the perfect ensemble, deciding on a hair style, getting a manicure—the action starts with all the pre-show primping. Throw your own pre-party, complete with hair and makeup stylist, while watching the pre-show festivities on TV. Treat your girlfriends (or boyfriends) to a professional makeup application . . . jungle red nails . . . or hair swept up into a gorgeous "do."

ICED WITH PIZZAZZ

One afternoon at Serendipity, we had the honor of hosting the famed fashionista Diana Vreeland, longtime editor in chief of *Vogue* magazine. She placed a simple order: iced Perrier water. The waiter, a bit unnerved to be serving such an elegant diva, poured sparkling water over ice and delivered it to her table. After taking a sip, Vreeland announced in her commanding tenor, "These are not Perrier ice cubes." I suppose you don't get to the top without paying attention to detail! In her honor, impress your guests by filling ice cube trays with sparkling water. Or, for a different kind of flourish, fill the ice cube trays with different color fruit juices (to use in sparkling water or iced tea) or coffee (for iced coffee or cappuccino).

ROCKING WITH OSCAR

1. "Over the Rainbow," Judy Garland
2. "Some Like It Hot," *Some Like It Hot* soundtrack
3. "Bennie and the Jets," Elton John
4. "Mrs. Robinson," Simon & Garfunkel
5. "Arms of a Woman," Amos Lee
6. "Pretty in Pink," The Psychedelic Furs
7. "Where Do the Children Play?" Cat Stevens
8. "Mon Amour, Mon Ami," Suzon (Virginie Ledoyen)
9. "As Time Goes By," *Casablanca* soundtrack
10. "Till the End of Time," Devotchka
11. "American Beauty," Thomas Newman
12. "Your Song," *Moulin Rouge* soundtrack
13. "All I Care About," *Chicago* soundtrack

NOMINEES FOR WORST DRESSED

Every year there are a number of Oscar-goers parading down the red carpet for whom you just cringe. Invite your friends to compete for the worst Oscar ensemble. You can also take it to the other extreme and ask everyone to come in his or her best black tie, or mix the two ideas and let each guest decide whether to go for best or worst dressed. Hopefully, it will be obvious which category they've chosen!

TV ETIQUETTE

To avoid potential problems between the "shushers" and the "talkers," try to set aside a space in your home where guests can go if they don't want to watch the Oscars (or not all three-plus hours of them). If you have two televisions, you can set them up in both rooms, but make it clear which room is a quiet zone and which is the free-for-all. You can make fun signs for the shushers' room such as: QUIET PLEASE, PROGRAM IN PROGRESS or ON AIR.

Cary Grant, Fred Astaire, and Sean Connery all wore boutonnieres. Who wouldn't want to join that club? To spread our feathers on Oscar night, there are few choices for the male peacocks of our species. Hundreds of years ago, men's fashion entered its current sober phase, limiting our ability to show off our colors to the size of a lapel. At Serendipity, we believe in displaying our colors no matter what. Dare to stray from the traditional boutonniere choices and try a calla lily, an orchid, a red dahlia, or a gardenia. To make your own:

❊ Cut the stem of the flower to about three inches. If you cut off any leaves, save them as greenery.

❊ Create a bed for the flower with a small amount of baby's breath and/or other greenery. Place the baby's breath between the greenery and the flower.

❊ Wrap all the stems together with green floral tape. If, however, you want to add some flair with ribbon, leave the stems unwrapped and go to the next step.

❊ Affix the greenery and baby's breath with a small amount of florist wire. Add enough floral tape to cover the wire and trim any loose stems from the greenery.

❊ Wrap the stems with ribbon (if using) and tie a bow at the bottom of the boutonniere. Use a 1/4-inch silk or satin ribbon for a touch of elegance.

❊ Keep the fresh flower boutonniere moist and cool until it is ready to be worn. Attach to your clothing with pearl-headed pins.

AUNT CHER, COUSIN MADONNA, AND GRANDPA BRANDO

Clip photos of celebrities from magazines, newspapers, or inexpensive used books. You can also download images of famous people from the Internet, and then Photoshop you and your family into the pictures. Buy cheap but tasteful picture frames and put a photo of a different celebrity in each one. Take the real family photos down from your walls and replace them with these fakes. When your guests arrive, give them a gallery tour: "Here we are on the cruise with George Clooney. There's Jack Nicholson laughing at my uncle's joke. Oh, and look at Barbra Streisand. She sang at my cousin's wedding." When the evening's over and it's time to go, invite each guest to select one of the pictures to take home.

KNOWING YOUR STARS

For entertainment during the commercials or when the show starts to drag, play Trivial Pursuit Silver Screen Edition. Or make up you own trivia game by going to the library and researching past Oscar winners in Robert Osborne's *Sixty-Five Years of Oscar: The Official History of the Academy of Motion Picture Arts & Sciences*. Ask guests to match movies with stars and the year the movie came out, or to match quotations and the movies that made them famous. "Oh, waiter. I'll be expecting some people. Champagne and a tin of caviar." (*Casablanca*). "Look at that. Look how she moves—it's like Jell-O on springs." (*Some Like It Hot*). A terrific source for this kind of information is IMDb.com. Prepare note cards with the question written on one side and the answer on the other. Take turns being the leader who reads out the questions while everyone else tries to guess the answer. Award prizes for the highest number of correct answers.

JUMPING IN THE OSCAR POOL

1. For each guest, print a copy of the list of Oscar nominees (available online at many sites, including Oscar.com).

2. Before the party, collect a dollar or other small amount of money from each participant to make a prize pool. Alternatively, you can award noncash prizes.

3. Before the awards show starts, make sure guests have completed their voting sheets and put their names at the top. You can either collect them all and keep a master list as the winners are announced, or each person can hold onto his or her own copy and keep score. How much do you trust your friends, especially if there are prizes at stake?

4. In Hollywood, Oscar winners receive gift baskets filled with designer goodies. As a prize for your guests, put together a knock-off gift basket with delicious treats, bath products, perfume, and makeup. For the guest who got the greatest number of wrong answers, give out a booby prize, such as a basket filled with gag products. If you collected a cash award, make a dramatic announcement and invite the winner to stand in front of the group and deliver a brief (set a time limit) acceptance speech.

CAVIAR DREAMS

The spurned wife of a Hollywood movie mogul took to bathing in caviar when her husband fell for a beautiful young actress. She had two reasons: 1) She believed the caviar would keep her skin soft; and 2) She paid for it with her husband's credit card, which made her even happier! Little did she know that her little act of vengeance would become a Hollywood craze in which starlets pay big bucks to be rubbed down with caviar. A recent Oscar gift basket included caviar eye cream!

BELUGA: A very expensive caviar with berries that range from pale gray to black.

GOLDEN OR IMPERIAL CAVIAR: This most expensive "caviar of the czars" is extremely rare and believed to come from albino fish or fish at least sixty years old.

OSETRA: A very expensive caviar that varies more in taste, color, and size than beluga or sevruga, with a fuller, nuttier flavor preferred by some connoisseurs.

PRESSED CAVIAR: Made from broken and more mature sturgeon eggs, this product is a combination of beluga, osetra, and sevruga.

RED CAVIAR: Not considered caviar by purists, these orange-colored eggs come from salmon roe and are much larger in size than genuine caviar.

SEVRUGA: Caviar that is somewhat less expensive and saltier than beluga or osetra.

TROUT EGGS: These smaller grained orange eggs are considered faux caviar.

BEST IN A SUPPORTING ROLE: BUCKWHEAT BLINI

1 envelope active dry yeast

1/4 cup lukewarm water

2 cups milk

2 cups buckwheat flour

1 teaspoon salt

3 eggs, separated

1 tablespoon unsalted butter, melted

1 teaspoon sugar

ACCOMPANIMENTS:

Melted butter, sour cream, and caviar

Soak the yeast in the lukewarm water and allow it to "proof" for 5 minutes (it should get bubbly on top).

Put 1 cup of the milk in a saucepan and heat to lukewarm. In a large mixing bowl, combine the yeast mixture with the cup of lukewarm milk. Sift together the buckwheat flour and the salt and stir the flour and salt mixture into the yeast and milk mixture to make a thick sponge. Cover the bowl with a clean dish towel and let the dough rise in a warm place for about 3 hours.

Heat the remaining cup of milk to lukewarm. In the saucepan, beat the 3 egg yolks well with the cup of lukewarm milk, melted butter, and sugar. Add this liquid mixture to the dough. The batter should be fairly thin; you may need to add as much as 1/2 cup of milk. Beat the batter well by hand and let it stand, covered, for half an hour.

Beat the 3 egg whites until stiff. Fold the beaten egg whites into the batter.

Heat and butter a griddle. Ladle the batter onto the griddle to form 3-inch blini.

Serve the blini with the melted butter, sour cream, and caviar.

NOTE: The blini may be made ahead of time and frozen. Allow them to cool, place wax paper between each one, stack them in a freezer bag, and store in the freezer. To reheat, place the blini in a toaster oven or regular oven at 250 degrees F until warm, 5 to 10 minutes.) Or, if you are pressed for time, you can buy prepared blini from your favorite gourmet store.

Makes 5 dozen small blini

RED CARPET GELATIN
WITH BALSAMIC BERRIES

**FOR THE STRAWBERRY
GELATIN:**

2 cups hulled strawberries

1 1/2 cups low-fat milk

1/2 cup heavy cream

1/3 to 1/2 cup sugar
(depending on sweetness
of strawberries)

1 vanilla bean, split
(optional)

1 envelope unflavored
gelatin

1/2 teaspoon vanilla extract

Puree the strawberries in a food processor until smooth. Pour the puree through a fine strainer, pressing with a rubber spatula to extract as much pulp and juice as possible and reserve.

Whisk the milk, cream, and sugar in a heavy medium saucepan. Scrape the vanilla bean (if using) from the pod into the milk mixture and whisk again. Sprinkle the gelatin over the mixture and let it stand until the gelatin softens, about 10 minutes. Whisk the mixture constantly over very low heat until the gelatin dissolves and the mixture is lukewarm, about 3 minutes (do not boil). Remove from heat.

Whisk in the pureed strawberries and the vanilla extract. Divide the mixture among 6 ramekins or decorative custard cups. Refrigerate until set, for at least 3 hours or overnight.

FOR THE BALSAMIC BERRIES:

3 1/2 cups sliced hulled strawberries

1/4 cup sugar

1 1/2 tablespoons balsamic vinegar (white balsamic is prettiest)

While the gelatin is setting, prepare the balsamic berries. In a medium bowl, combine the sliced strawberries, sugar, and balsamic vinegar. Refrigerate for at least 1 hour but not more than 3 hours.

To serve, remove the gelatin from the refrigerator and spoon a generous topping of balsamic berries over each cup.

NOTE: If you have any balsamic berries left over, they will keep in the refrigerator for a few days and are a delicious topping for vanilla ice cream.

Makes 8 servings

TSARINA CHAMPAGNE COCKTAIL

1 sugar cube

1 ounce chilled pomegranate juice

3 ounces chilled Champagne or sparkling wine

Several pomegranate seeds (optional)

Place a sugar cube in the bottom of a Champagne glass. Pour in the pomegranate juice, followed by the Champagne or sparkling wine. Drop a few pomegranate seeds into the glass as a garnish (if using). Serve immediately.

VARIATION: For a nonalcoholic drink, substitute sparkling apple cider or sparkling grape juice for the Champagne or sparkling wine.

Makes 1 serving

CHAPTER THREE

SWINGING BIRTHDAY FLINGS:

FROM PAINT DRIPPING TO CHOCOLATE DIPPING

At Serendipity, we firmly believe that it's fun to be frivolous. And what better excuse could there be for acting frivolous than a birthday? We have such a reputation for embracing frivolity that generations of East Side kids have chosen Serendipity for their birthday parties. And countless stars of stage and screen have also used our restaurant to host their birthday celebrations.

Just a couple of decades ago, I kept the antique wooden hat rack at Serendipity full of chapeaus that I was creating for stores like Bergdorf Goodman and Bendel's. Brooke Shields modeled my hats when she was an ingenue, just after her film debut in *Pretty Baby*. She continues to be a loyal customer; she and one of her girls celebrated a mother/daughter birthday in grand serendipitous style.

In fact, many famous mother/daughter duos have marked milestones at Serendipity over the years. For her fifty-second birthday, Jackie Onassis lunched with her daughter, Caroline, who gave her mom an unframed woodcut print and a lace-and-satin lingerie case. Jackie reciprocated by buying Caroline a baseball cap made of antique upholstery chintz from the restaurant's boutique. Serendipity has always been a family affair when it comes to birthdays. Beyoncé recently celebrated her twenty-second birthday with us, along with her boyfriend Jay-Z and her sister Solange. Other Serendpity birthday celebrations have included sundaes for Warren Beatty and Annette Bening to indulge their son Ben and a father/daughter birthday for Ron Howard and Bryce Dallas-Howard.

No matter whom you choose to celebrate with, birthdays are a time to remind ourselves that life is about more than just work. Remember what it's like to be a child again—throw some paint around or dip your body in chocolate. Whatever games you play or activities you organize, it's important to be attuned to your own party. Just relax and enjoy the time spent with friends.

PARTY MENU

SALSA AND CHIPS

TIMELESS SUCCOTASH
(page 40)

MINI MEAT LOAF "CUPCAKES"
(page 41)

MINI BBQ CHICKEN POT PIES
(page 42)

STAR-FOR-A-DAY
CHOCOLATE CAKES
(page 44)

LEMONADE OR
SHIRLEY TEMPLES
(page 43)

COFFEE

SURPRISES ALL AROUND

If you are able to pull off a surprise party (which is never easy), this is a little added surprise. Using a photo of the birthday honoree (a face close-up is best) enlarge the photo to the scale of a real face, make color reproductions, and cut out and mount on foam core. Make holes for eyes with an Exacto knife and glue a dowel onto the back of the mask in order to hold it. After all the guests have arrived, distribute these masks to everyone. Just before the surprise victim comes in, dim the lights, ask all to put on the masks, and surprise! When the lights come up, the birthday boy or girl will be surrounded by more than a few familiar faces.

EXHIBITIONISTS ONLY

At Serendipity, we collect all kinds of artifacts, such as a 6-foot-tall clock we saved from the wrecking ball, Andy Warhol's effigy, a Pegasus from a Mobil gas station sign, a legendary espresso machine, Victorian prints from a Paris hotel, street signs, and many more. Collecting personal artifacts is a uniquely meaningful way to celebrate the birth of a friend, a spouse, a sibling, or a child.

Put together a wacky museum exhibit dedicated to the honoree, especially for a big birthday like forty, fifty, or sixty. Display the assorted artifacts on tables or hang them on walls like a gallery space. Accompany these historical objects with official-sounding titles and descriptions that you might see in an art museum. Pair the silliest items with the most serious captions. Here's a list to get you started: first toothbrush, lock of baby hair, high school English paper, copy of résumé, love note, expired passport, prom dress. A label might read: ANDY WARHOL'S SHOE AD FOR BENDEL'S, PEN AND INK, CIRCA 1955 or MARY SMITH'S CORSAGE, JUNIOR PROM, DRIED ROSES AND BABY'S BREATH, CIRCA 1972.

SWEET SIXTEEN CHOCOLATE SPA PARTY

Who doesn't like the idea of drifting in a sea of chocolate? When it comes to chocolate, our mantra is: "Eat it, drink it, wear it." And now that science has confirmed that chocolate contains antioxidants that help soothe skin and stimulate circulation, we can indulge in chocolate's intoxicating aroma while soaking up its many health benefits. Set up a chocolate spa in your home for a special sixteen-year-old—or for anyone who wants to feel like a sixteen-year-old again.

✳ Along with buckets of warm water, stock your spa with Serendipity's best: try our Chocolate Bubble Bath, Chocolate Body Icing moisturizer, and Frrrozen Hot Chocolate Foot Cream. Add your other favorite chocolate lotions, wraps, shampoos, scrubs, and bath gels.

✳ Make your own chocolate bubble bath by combining 3 ounces of unsweetened cocoa powder and 1/3 cup of milk. Under running bath water, add the cocoa/milk mixture plus 1 cup of unscented bubble bath, and soak in a chocolate sea.

✳ Set up television trays with everything necessary for manicures, plus a makeup mirror accompanied by brown-hued eye shadows, bronze lipsticks, and so on.

✳ If the budget permits, hire a professional masseuse or manicurist for administering the chocolate cure.

✳ For guests who are waiting for a spa treatment, create your own cocoa bar, including chocolate spice tea, hot chocolate, and Frrrozen Hot Chocolate.

✳ Make chocolate body paint: In a small pan over medium heat, warm 1/4 cup of heavy cream and pour it over a bowl containing 2 1/2 ounces of milk or dark chocolate, broken into small pieces. Stir until smooth and let cool slightly. Use new paintbrushes, preferably small ones, and be creative!

✳ For a sweet party favor, choose from a mini box of chocolates, cocoa lip balm, or perfume.

CRASHING ELOISE STYLE

Like Eloise, we would rawther live at the Plaza, but since the hotel has been turned into luxury apartments, we must find another place to crash for a special birthday night. Everyone appreciates the convenience of hotel living, so for an intimate party, book a room or a suite at your favorite hotel. Invite four or five friends to come in their pajamas for a slumber party. Bring lots of drinks and junk food to munch on while you watch old movies, have pillow fights, and play Truth or Dare. For younger kids, organize a themed scavenger hunt and scour the hotel for clues and prizes. Eloise, the mischievous child character created by Kay Thompson, is a perfect theme for this kind of scavenger hunt. Use a photocopier to enlarge images from the Eloise books and tape them to the wall of your hotel room. To save money, order pizza from a local pizzeria instead of room service. Or prepare your own Eloise menu with Teeny Weenies (tiny hot dogs), Skipperdee Sandwiches (peanut butter and jelly), Kiddie Kar Kocktails (ginger ale), and Supersonic Sherbet (rainbow sherbet). But if Skipperdee gets hungry, it's okay to order raisins from room service!

Speaking of scavenger hunts and menus, Serendipity's menus (and pieces of the menu) used to disappear all the time only to turn up later as popular items in scavenger hunts. Legend has it that there was a dormitory bathroom at Yale that was wallpapered entirely with Serendipity menus! We finally had to have the menus laminated, so we could keep enough around for our customers.

LET THEM ENTERTAIN YOU

Looking for a way to throw your own birthday party without a lot of fuss? Invite your friends to a potluck picnic in the park. If you are fortunate enough to live in a city or town that organizes free concerts in the park, pick a night when classical music or opera is on the schedule. Bring the main course and a cake, and ask others to contribute a bottle of wine or a simple side dish. If you'd prefer a fancier gathering, ask for help and bring a bunch of matching chairs in a bright color. Arrange the chairs in a large circle to cordon off your area for the party. If you know it's going to be a popular event, where the audience crowds together on blankets, make sure to get there early to mark off your territory and tell your friends in advance exactly where you'll be. Set up a small folding table for your buffet supper, and voilà, an instant party, including entertainment!

PLAYING WITH PAINT THE POLLOCK WAY

Surely serendipity played a role in Jackson Pollock's innovative painting style. He was known for flinging, dripping, pouring, and splattering paint on a canvas on the floor as he circled the canvas in an energetic dance.

1. You will need washable paints (like poster paint) and the largest size canvas that fits your budget and the dimensions of the room you plan to use for creating the masterpiece.

2. Collect some or all of the following: empty tin cans (with tops removed), hardened paintbrushes, old turkey basters, plastic squeeze bottles, Popsicle sticks.

3. Clear a large space in the middle of a room that you don't mind getting messy (consider the garage or a rec room, or outside in the yard).

4. Cover the space with a tarp, newspapers, or a large piece of plastic and lay the canvas on top. Either weight the corners of the canvas (again, with items you don't mind getting paint on) or tape down the edges with masking tape. Make sure there is a two-foot clearance between the edge of the floor covering and the edges of the canvas. The canvas can also be taped to a wall, but you will need something larger than the canvas to protect the wall from wayward paint.

5. For the guests who wish to paint, provide them with smocks or garbage bags perforated with arm and head holes, so their party clothes will be protected. (Even with protection, clothes may get a bit splattered, so encourage guests to come in their "play" clothes.)

6. Provide as many colors of washable paint as possible and a number of options for paint application. For example, use a can opener to poke a hole in the bottom of the empty cans. When someone is ready to start, pour paint into the can and it will immediately begin dripping over the canvas. Or fill turkey basters or squeeze bottles with paint and use them to squirt designs onto the canvas. Or dip hardened paintbrushes or Popsicle sticks in paint and fling them onto the canvas.

7. For those guests who want to make wearable art, distribute white T-shirts for throwing paint at and on, and they can take home their very own Pollock. This project requires paints that won't wash out of clothes (such as liquid latex, which also happens to dry quickly).

8. At the end of the party, present the floor-sized Pollock masterpiece to the birthday boy or girl as a souvenir. (If the paint has not fully dried, leave the canvas on the floor until it dries completely and deliver it at a later time.)

STARSTRUCK

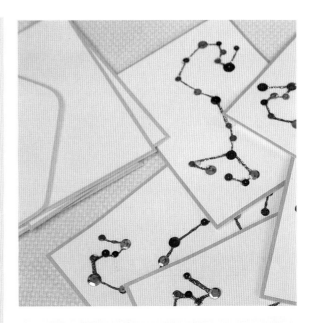

Our beloved hostess Grace doubles as Serendipity's in-house mystic. It's always fun looking to the stars for answers. Plan an astrological birthday for your spouse, partner, or best friend.

INVITATIONS: Draw or trace the symbol of different zodiac signs on card stock and decorate them with glitter.

CENTERPIECE: Before the party, find out the exact birth date and time of the honored boy or girl and have a star chart done. Mount the star chart on poster board or foam board and place it on an easel in the center of the table.

PLACE CARDS: For each guest, write a horoscope on one side of the place card and his or her name on the other side. You can either clip horoscopes from newspapers or fashion magazines or play astrologer and make up whimsical forecasts.

GAME: Ask guests to walk around the table and select the card they think best matches their personality and then sit in that spot. Turn over all the cards at the same time and realign your stars (rearrange the seats according to the correct astrological signs).

GUESTS: Be conscious of your guests. Some star signs are more—or less—compatible with others. Put the right two together and you could create a match made in heaven.

HAPPY BIRTHDAY TO YOU

1. "Birthday," The Beatles
2. "Ages of You," R.E.M.
3. "How You've Grown," 10,000 Maniacs
4. "Imagine," John Lennon
5. "Free Bird," Lynyrd Skynyrd
6. "Happy Birthday, Mr. President," Marilyn Monroe
7. "One of These Days," Doves
8. "Love and Memories," O.A.R.
9. "You Make Me Feel So Young," Frank Sinatra
10. "Night Becomes Day," Citizen Cope
11. "Dancing Queen," Abba
12. "Surprise Surprise," The Rolling Stones
13. "Where Have All the Good Times Gone," The Kinks
14. "Sweet Child O' Mine," Guns N' Roses
15. "Naïve," The Kooks

TIMELESS SUCCOTASH

**3 tablespoons
unsalted butter**

1 shallot, finely chopped

**2 (10-ounce) packages
frozen cut green beans**

**2 (10-ounce) packages
frozen sweet corn**

**2 (10-ounce) packages
frozen baby lima beans**

2 teaspoons salt

**1/2 teaspoon freshly
ground pepper**

Juice of 1 lime

**1 teaspoon finely
grated lime zest**

Melt the butter in a large, nonstick skillet over medium heat. When it stops foaming, add the shallot and cook until softened, about 3 minutes.

Carefully add the green beans, corn, and lima beans to the pan (frozen vegetables can sometimes splatter), and season with salt and pepper. Stirring often, cook the vegetables until they're crisp-tender, about 6 minutes. The water from the frozen vegetables will steam them from the inside while you sauté them, so you don't need to add extra water to the pan.

Remove the pan from the heat, stir in the lime juice and lime zest, and season to taste with additional salt and pepper. Serve warm.

Makes 8 servings

MINI MEAT LOAF "CUPCAKES"

FOR THE MEAT LOAF:

1 pound lean ground beef

1/2 cup seasoned bread crumbs

1 cup grated Monterey Jack cheese

3 tablespoons ketchup

1 egg

1/2 teaspoon celery salt

1/4 teaspoon freshly ground pepper

FOR THE POTATO "FROSTING":

3 cups mashed potatoes

Blue, yellow, and pink food coloring

Preheat the oven to 375 degrees F. Line muffin tins with 12 foil liners.

In a large bowl, gently mix the ground beef, bread crumbs, cheese, ketchup, egg, celery salt, and pepper until well combined. Divide the mixture evenly among the lined cups, filling each about three-quarters full. Place the muffin tins on cookie sheets and bake the cupcakes for about 15 minutes, or until the meat is no longer pink.

To make the potato "frosting," divide the mashed potatoes among three small bowls. Add a few drops of blue, yellow, or pink food coloring to each bowl and blend to create pastel frostings. Spread a generous dollop of colored topping on each cupcake.

Makes 12 "cupcakes"

BBQ CHICKEN POT PIES

2 cups all-purpose flour, plus more for rolling

1/2 teaspoon baking soda

1/2 teaspoon salt

1/2 cup grated Cheddar cheese

4 tablespoons minced chives

12 tablespoons (1 1/2 sticks) cold unsalted butter, cut into 1/2-inch pieces, plus more for greasing pans

6 tablespoons buttermilk

1/4 cup chopped chives (optional)

3/4 cup barbecue sauce (purchased or homemade, see page 112)

1 pound cooked chicken meat, finely chopped

To prepare the crust, combine the flour, baking soda, and salt in a large mixing bowl. Stir in the cheese and minced chives. With a pastry blender or two knives (or in a food processor), cut the butter into the flour mixture until it resembles coarse meal. Make a well in the center of the mixture and pour in the buttermilk. Gently fold in the buttermilk until the dough starts to come together. Remove the dough from the bowl and place on a lightly floured surface, sprinkling with additional flour as necessary. Gently knead into a smooth ball. Flatten the ball into a disk, wrap it in plastic wrap, and refrigerate for at least 30 minutes.

Preheat the oven to 350 degrees F. Lightly grease a muffin tin or mini-muffin tin. To prepare the filling, combine the chopped chicken and barbecue sauce in a medium bowl, thoroughly moistening the chicken with the sauce.

After removing the dough from the refrigerator, allow it to soften for several minutes on the countertop. Break off balls of dough for each pie's crust, about the size of golf balls for a regular muffin tin or about the size of Ping-Pong balls for a mini-muffin tin. Roll out each ball of dough to a thickness of 1/8 inch or less, gently drape it inside the muffin tin, and lightly press it into place. Flute the edges of the dough as you wish. Fill each pie to the top with chicken.

Bake the pies for 10 to 15 minutes, or until the crust turns golden around the edges. Remove from the oven and let cool in the pan for about 5 minutes.

Garnish with the chopped chives and serve either warm or at room temperature.

Makes 12 regular muffin-size pies or 32 mini pot pies

PASTEL-PAINTED MARSHMALLOWS

4 to 5 drops food coloring

1/2 (10-ounce) bag or 20 large marshmallows

Place a double layer of paper towels on a cookie sheet or counter. Add 4 to 5 drops of any color food coloring to 1/3 cup water in individual small shallow bowls, and mix well. Roll the marshmallows around in the bowls until saturated with color. Gently spear each marshmallow with a toothpick, being careful to pierce it as little as possible. Place the marshmallows on the paper towels to dry. Repeat with the remaining marshmallows.

Makes 20 marshmallows

CLASSIC SHIRLEY TEMPLE

6 ounces ginger ale

3 ounces orange juice

1/2 to 1 tablespoon grenadine

Maraschino cherry

Slice of orange

Combine the ginger ale, orange juice, and grenadine in a glass filled with ice, and garnish with a maraschino cherry and a slice of orange.

NOTE: For extra flair, decorate the glass with a miniature paper umbrella or plastic cocktail monkey.

VARIATION: For an alcoholic version, add a shot of rum to the glass.

Makes 1 serving

STAR-FOR-A-DAY CHOCOLATE CAKES

8 tablespoons (1 stick) unsalted butter, at room temperature

1 pound dark brown sugar

4 ounces unsweetened chocolate, melted

3 eggs

1 teaspoon vanilla extract

1 1/4 cups sifted cake flour

Pinch of salt

1/2 cup sour cream

2 teaspoons baking soda

1 cup boiling water

Preheat the oven to 350 degrees F.

Line 2 tins that each have 6 star shapes (with 1/2-cup capacity) with parchment paper. To cut the parchment paper to the correct size, turn over the pan to trace the outline of one star onto parchment paper. Once one is cut out, you can use that as a template to cut out the rest. Lightly spray the interiors with non-stick baking spray or lightly grease each pan with melted butter using a pastry brush. Dust each pan with flour, knocking out any excess flour. Place the parchment cutouts into the bottom of each pan, lightly spray or grease the parchment with melted butter, and then dust with flour. (To make removing the cakes as easy as possible, use silicone pans if available.)

In a large bowl of an electric mixer, using the paddle attachment, cream together the butter and sugar at medium speed until the mixture is very light in color, about 5 minutes. With the mixer turned off, add the chocolate and resume mixing, using a spatula to scrape down the sides of the bowl. Add the eggs one at a time, followed by the vanilla, mixing well after each addition.

Combine the flour with the salt in a medium bowl. In a small bowl, whisk together the sour cream, baking soda, and boiling water until there are no lumps.

Alternating between the sour cream mixture and the flour and salt mixture, add half of each to the chocolate and butter mixture and mix at medium speed until just combined.

Pour the batter into the cake pans so they are no more than half filled. Bake for about 20 minutes, or until a toothpick inserted in the center of the cake comes out clean. Remove the pans to a cooling rack and

allow to cool for at least 30 minutes before unmolding.

Frost the cakes once they have reached room temperature. White Chocolate Sour Cream Frosting (see below) or divinity (page 119) makes a fabulous frosting for these rich and decadent chocolate cakes.

NOTE: Invite your guests to design individual masterpieces they can then devour. Provide everyone with a small bowl of frosting, and arrange colored marshmallows (page 43), assorted sprinkles, candies, and other decorations in the center of the table. Distribute the unadorned chocolate cakes and watch their imaginations run wild.

Makes 12 small cakes

WHITE CHOCOLATE SOUR CREAM FROSTING

10 ounces white chocolate, coarsely chopped

1 cup sour cream

Melt the chocolate in the top of a double boiler or in a microwave for 10 seconds at a time, until just melted. Stir in the sour cream and mix until just combined. Use the frosting immediately. If the frosting becomes too stiff, return it to the double boiler or microwave for a few seconds to soften.

Makes about 2 cups

CHAPTER FOUR

DOWN THE RABBIT HOLE FOR SUNDAY TEA:

MAD HATTER MIX AND MATCH

When you descend Serendipity's spiral staircase from the restaurant's Victorian parlor, you may feel like Alice falling down the rabbit hole when you land in a be-Tiffany-ed fantasy with curios crammed in every corner. Your sense of scale is thrown off by an enormous clock and a miniature Andy Warhol. Perfect for a Mad Hatter's tea party! The restaurant, in fact, used to serve high tea, featuring a large silver urn filled with hibiscus tea, pink petits fours, and watercress sandwiches. And we once gave a tea party for charity and offered crumpets, scones, miniature banana-nut muffins with whipped butter, curried shrimp salad with chutney on golden raisin bread, deviled chicken and ham on double seeded rye, lemon and orange sponge cakes—and that was just the beginning!

Even if you're not inclined to produce such an extensive spread, and your home does not look like Wonderland, all you need for a lively tea party is some zany decor and imaginative food. Start by choosing an unusual setting. The March Hare and the Hatter were fortunate to have a table set out under a tree in front of their house. If you are lucky enough to have a yard or a terrace, by all means set up your table outside beneath a tree. If not, grow your own tree by affixing a large poster of a tree or by tacking the word *TREE* in giant letters on the wall closest to the dining table. Read on for more ideas for "maddening" your table.

Party Menu

HANGOVER HELPER OMELET
(page 55)

ASSORTMENT OF TEA
SANDWICHES (pages 56–57)

SCONES WITH BUTTER,
JAM, & CLOTTED CREAM

SAY WHAT YOU MEAN, EAT
WITH YOUR HANDS ANGEL
FOOD CAKE (page 58)
OR PETITS FOURS

ORANGE JUICE OR MIMOSAS

VARIETY OF TEAS
(page 51)

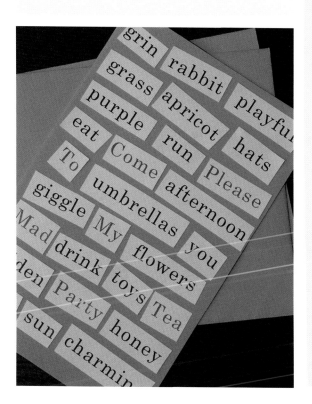

A NOTE FROM THE JABBERWOCKY

Taking a page from Lewis Carroll's book, we like to make invitations from a jumble of words. You never know what serendipitous joys may spring from nonsense! Using your computer, a set of stamps, or a calligraphy set, compose a nonsensical series of merry words, such as those you might conjure during a sunny afternoon tea party or find in Alice in Wonderland, leaving space between each word. At the end of your composition, include the actual invitation's message, such as "Please Come to My Mad Tea Party." Cut out each of the words and glue them haphazardly on the front of your invitation, making sure to include the message, but spaced apart and on different lines. At first glance, it may appear to be gobbledygook, but the eye will soon pick out the message. Using questions like "Who Are You?"—inspired by Alice's encounter with the caterpillar—lends a particularly whimsical note. Or write your own Alice-inspired poem such as this one:

Please come for "much of a muchness"
Dine with not much of a Duchess
A very important date
It's never too late
To feel mad and sip tea
With serendipity.

A TOPSY-TURVY TABLE

To set a whimsical table, mix and match tea-cups, saucers, napkins, and tea towels. Include a wide variety of styles, ranging from vintage to contemporary. You can usually score inexpensive treasures at flea markets or garage sales. Set the table for high tea with a large urn in the center or a grouping of quirky teapots. For a different and stunning centerpiece, construct a teacup tower, being sure to use the largest cups for the base. Or serve tea in wineglasses with tags that say DRINK ME. (Make sure the tea is not boiling hot.) For napkin rings, make bows out of red licorice strings or use cookie cutters in assorted shapes. To encourage your guests to mix and mingle, try this dice trick: Make oversized dice by taking plain white gift-box cubes and affixing black dots to each side as shown. Set the dice on the table, and, after each course, ask one of your guests to take a roll. Whatever number pops up on the dice is the number of seats he or she must move to the right, thereby taking a seat next to new neighbors.

EGG-CRACKING MASTERY

At Serendipity, we used to feature an omelet bar downstairs. Each diner could walk up to the bar and choose from a variety of fillings for a customized omelet. One day in the 1970s, James Beard, the towering bow-tied impresario of American cooking, came in to try our omelets. After quietly observing Calvin and Patch and me, he winked and whispered in my ear, "Let me give you a couple of tips." We were invited to his handsome townhouse in Greenwich Village for private omelet-making classes! We figured we'd have to mortgage the restaurant to pay for lessons with the master, but how could we say no? The classes were scheduled, and we appeared at the appointed hour. "It's all in the wrist," he said repeatedly like a wise piano teacher. We spent hours cracking eggs, until each of us had filled a whole crate with shells. When all was said and done, Mr. Beard never sent us a bill. What a generous teacher he was after all!

To transform your dining room into an omelet bar, all you need is a hot plate, spatulas, melted butter, a large bowl of beaten eggs, and lots of small bowls with various fillings chopped and ready to go. Mushrooms, peppers, onions, ham, Cheddar cheese, and bacon are classic fillings. You can also experiment with more unusual ingredients like leeks, fennel, shallots, crabmeat, and Brie cheese. Hire someone to work the station or let one of your friends "eggsplore" his or her chefly talents.

Ideal water temperatures for infusing: Black tea (212 degrees F), oolong tea (194 to 212 degrees F), green tea (176 to 185 degrees F), white tea (176 to 185 degrees F), and herbal teas (170 degrees F).

1. Green Butterfly is a green tea with the sweet aroma of rose petals. This tea is picked by hand in early spring and turns the water a beautiful soft jade color.

2. Silver Needle Jasmine is a white tea with a fruity aroma, notes of honeydew melon, and a downy appearance. It has a high concentration of polyphenols (antioxidants that help fight cancer-causing free radicals and heart disease).

3. White Pearl is a green tea, rolled into soft, irregular pearl shapes. It appears white and downy and has a mellow, earthy flavor with a lasting note of chocolate.

4. Pu-erh Tea, named after a county in China, is a green tea with a strong, rich, earthy flavor. This very expensive tea can be purchased after it has aged for ten to fifty years.

5. Rooibos is an herbal tea with a sweet, nutty flavor derived from the Rooibos plant that grows only in South Africa.

6. Lemon Verbena is an herbal tea with a clean, fresh lemony taste that helps strengthen the nervous system and aids digestion.

7. Honey Phoenix is an oolong tea with a strong honey aroma and taste. It is picked and processed by hand, and the leaves appear twisted into wiry shapes.

8. Chrysanthemum is an herbal tea known for its healing properties, and it is especially useful for treating fevers. This tea has a delicate, clear, slightly sweet, refreshing taste.

9. Cardamom Chai Tea is an herbal tea that contains star anise, cloves, and bright safflower petals that impart a rich, spicy character to this caffeine-free infusion.

10. Monkey Picked is an oolong tea that was indeed once picked by monkeys. Now hand-picked by humans, this tea turns a deep golden brown when brewed and releases a bitter smoke and sweet fruit flavor.

ALICE, THE MAD HATTER, AND MARCH HARE MAKE A PROPER TEA

1. "Use loose tea leaves," said Alice. "There isn't any," said the March Hare." They are far superior to bags," said Alice.

2. "Fill the kettle with cold water and bring it to the right temperature," said Alice. "It's all the same," said the March Hare. "No, it depends on what kind of fancy tea you have," said Alice. "Once the water boils or reaches the correct point, turn it off to brew the tea," said the March Hare. "I think you might do something better with the time," said Alice. "If the water boils too long, it loses oxygen and the tea tastes murky," said the March Hare.

3. "Place 1 heaping teaspoon of leaves (per cup) into an earthenware pot, if one is available," said the March Hare. "Then it wasn't very civil of you to offer it," said Alice angrily. "Or pour it right into the porcelain serving pot with the leaves in the pot and use a strainer or tea infuser," said the March Hare.

4. "Pour hot water directly on the leaves," said the March Hare. "How dreadfully savage!" exclaimed Alice. "Cover the teapot and let steep for 3 to 6 minutes, depending on the size of the tea leaves," said Alice. "Exactly so, small leaves steep the shortest, and large ones the longest," said the March Hare.

5. "If the tea was steeped in the earthenware pot, transfer to a porcelain pot, as that will retain heat better," said the March Hare. "I don't know what you mean," said Alice. "In China, they pour out the first infusion to wash the tea and drink the second and further infusions, but here it's always tea time, and we've no time to wash the things between whiles," said the Hatter.

6. "Strain the tea into cups and serve with lemon, milk, sugar, or honey if desired," said Alice. "I want a clean cup," interrupted the Hatter: "Let's all move one place on."

SERENDIPITY IN A BOX

Conceptual artist Joseph Cornell became famous for creating small boxes that resembled surreal curio cabinets. He would collect a seemingly random group of objects and affix them in a box, creating a bewitching piece of art that sparks the imagination. Serendipity is like a giant Joseph Cornell box. Our townhouse may be small and boxlike, but it is stuffed with objects we have purposefully and lovingly collected over the years. Why not make your own Cornell-inspired treasure at home? Create something rich in meaning and mystery that only appears to consist of objects thrown together serendipitously.

As the poet Charles Simic once said, Cornell's boxes "are dreams that a child would know. Dreams in which objects are renamed and invested with imaginary lives. A pebble becomes a human being. Two sticks leaning against each other make a house."

1. Troll through antique stores, art supply stores, flea markets, or yard sales looking for a variety of open boxes. An old cigar box without the top, for example, is ideal.

2. Collect trinkets and oddities from the same sources or your home: marbles, Ping-Pong balls, old postage stamps, paper clips, wire, mismatched holiday decor or art supplies, kitschy shot glasses, seashells, thimbles, pipes, etc.

3. Gather a variety of print materials (as these will be cut up, don't include anything you want to save): magazines with unusual graphics, maps (especially astronomical or topographical maps), holiday cards, pages from old books with weird text or diagrams, etc.

4. Put your materials in the center of a work table with craft glue. Starting with the flatter materials made of paper, choose a background for the box and glue those down.

5. Secure the larger three-dimensional objects inside the box. The idea is to decorate the box with objects and words that will invite observers to imagine and dream.

SCISSORS CAN MAKE POETRY

This idea originated with the Romanian dadaist poet Tristan Tzara. Gather up a mix of magazines and newspapers (ranging from the cerebral *New Yorker* to scientific or technical journals) and cut out lots of text, including complete lines, short phrases, and individual words. Or you can type up your own mix of words on a computer, print them out, and cut them into separate strips. Whichever method you choose, fold the strips in half, so the words are hidden. Place them into a punch bowl (or a large "Mad Hat"), and give it a good shake. Let your guests pick out a number of strips (around ten), and they can either string the lines together as a poem in the order they were chosen or rearrange the lines as they wish. Everyone then takes turns reading the "mad" poems out loud.

MARCHING TO MADNESS

1. "Mysterious Ways," U2
2. "Sunday Sunny Mill Valley Groove Day," Frank Black
3. "Scarborough Fair/Canticle," Simon & Garfunkel
4. "Sunday," Sia
5. "Who Wants to Live Forever," Queen
6. "Fool," Cat Power
7. "This Must Be the Place (Naive Melody)," Talking Heads
8. "Saint Simon," The Shins
9. "Girl," Beck
10. "City Love," John Mayer
11. "Don't Stand So Close to Me," The Police
12. "Time and Time Again," Counting Crows
13. "Sing Me Back Home," Grateful Dead
14. "Marching Bands of Manhattan," Death Cab for Cutie
15. "Take It Easy," The Eagles
16. "Love Today," MIKA
17. "Shine on You Crazy Diamond," Pink Floyd
18. "Lucy in the Sky with Diamonds," The Beatles

HANGOVER HELPER OMELET

2 eggs

1 1/2 tablespoons
unsalted butter

1 to 2 ounces grated
Cheddar cheese

2 teaspoons minced
jalapeño pepper

Salt and pepper

2 teaspoons minced fresh
herbs (optional)

Beat the eggs with a whisk or a fork for 20 to 30 seconds. In an 8-inch nonstick skillet, melt the butter over medium heat. The butter will start to foam, and the pan is ready when the foam starts to subside. Pour in the eggs and let them set for 2 to 3 seconds. Sprinkle the cheese and jalapeño pepper evenly over the eggs. Cook for 20 to 30 seconds or until just golden, tilting the pan and rolling the egg mixture toward the opposite side of the pan, and using a spatula to help push and keep it together. Keeping the pan tilted at a slight angle away from you, gradually flip the pan so that the omelet flips over onto itself, folding in half. Slide the omelet onto a plate and serve. Season with salt and pepper to taste and garnish with the fresh herbs, if using.

Makes 1 serving

CHICKEN NUT-TEA SANDWICHES

Broth or water

2 whole boneless chicken breasts (about 1 1/2 pounds), skin on and cut in half

3/4 cup mayonnaise

1/3 cup minced shallot

2 teaspoons lemon juice

1 teaspoon celery salt

Freshly ground pepper

24 very thin slices white bread

1/2 cup walnuts, toasted

Fill a deep 12-inch skillet with enough broth or water to cover the chicken breasts. Bring the broth or water to a boil and add the chicken breasts in a single layer. Reduce the heat and poach the chicken at a bare simmer, turning once, for 7 minutes. Remove the skillet from the heat and cool the chicken in its cooking liquid for 20 minutes. Discard the skin from the chicken and chop the meat finely. In a medium bowl, stir together the chicken, 1/2 cup of the mayonnaise, the shallot, lemon juice, celery salt, and pepper to taste.

Assemble 12 sandwiches by spooning 2 tablespoons of the chicken salad between two slices of bread. Gently press each sandwich together. Using a 2-inch round cookie cutter, cut 2 rounds from each sandwich. Chop the walnuts in a food processor until the consistency resembles coarse meal. Place the ground nuts on a small plate. Use the remaining 1/4 cup of mayonnaise to coat the edges of the sandwich rounds. Roll the coated edges in the walnut meal.

NOTE: These sandwiches may be prepared 2 hours in advance. Wrap them in plastic or cover them with moist tea towels, and refrigerate until ready to serve.

Makes 24 sandwiches

DORMOUSE CRESS AND
EGG SANDWICHES

6 hard-boiled eggs, peeled and mashed

2 bunches watercress, washed, stems removed, and coarsely chopped

1/4 cup chopped fresh chives

3/4 cup mayonnaise

Salt and pepper

1/2 teaspoon paprika

2 loaves thinly sliced bread

1/4 cup chopped fresh dill, parsley, or a combination of both

In a medium mixing bowl, combine the eggs, watercress, and chives with just enough mayonnaise (approximately 1/2 cup) to moisten and bind the mixture. Season with salt, pepper, and paprika, and mix well. Cut the bread slices into interesting shapes, using whatever cookie cutters you have on hand. Spread the egg and watercress mixture onto half the bread shapes and top each with the matching shapes. Lightly spread the remaining 1/4 cup mayonnaise around the outside edges of the sandwiches. Roll each sandwich in the chopped herbs.

NOTE: These sandwiches may be prepared 2 hours in advance. Wrap them in plastic or cover them with moist tea towels, and refrigerate until ready to serve.

Makes 24 to 36 sandwiches

SAY WHAT YOU MEAN, EAT WITH YOUR HANDS ANGEL FOOD CAKE

1 cup cake flour

1/4 teaspoon salt

1 cup egg whites (from 7 to 8 large eggs)

1 teaspoon cream of tartar

1 teaspoon vanilla extract

1 1/4 cups sugar

4 different food colors (preferably neon colors, like hot pink, electric green, etc.)

Preheat the oven to 325 degrees F. Cut a piece of parchment paper to fit the bottom of an angel food cake pan (preferably one that has legs and a removable bottom). Sift the flour 4 times. In a large mixing bowl, stir the salt into the egg whites and whip with an electric mixer until the mixture becomes frothy. Sprinkle the cream of tartar over the egg whites and continue to beat until they hold soft, moist peaks. Fold in the vanilla. Gradually beat the sugar, 2 tablespoons at a time, into the egg white mixture, Sift a small amount of the flour over the egg white mixture and gently fold it in. Continue until the entire cup of flour has been added. Very gently pour the cake batter into 4 medium bowls. Add several drops of food coloring into each bowl and gently blend it into the batter. Do not overmix. You want to keep the mixture airy and light.

Put a large spoonful of cake batter of one color into the cake pan. Cycling through the other colors of batter, fill the pan one scoop at a time until all the batter has been added. Use a butter knife to gently make 4 crisscrosses through the batter. Do not stir or make too many slashes. Bake the cake for approximately 1 hour, or until the top springs back when touched lightly.

When the cake is done, invert it and allow it to cool for 1 hour. Using a dull knife, circle around the edges of the cake to loosen it from the pan. Invert the cake onto a plate. Serve it to your guests with instructions to grab a handful, pull, and eat!

NOTE: This can also be made using an angel food cake mix. Just follow the instructions on the box and add food coloring as described above.

Makes 6 to 10 servings

QUEEN OF HEARTS RUSSIAN TEA

1 cup Tang (or other powdered orange drink mix)

1 1/2 cups sugar

1/2 cup instant iced tea mix

1 teaspoon ground cinnamon

1 teaspoon ground cloves

Mix all the ingredients together and store the mixture in an airtight container. When ready to use, blend 2 teaspoons of the mixture with 1 cup of boiling water for each serving.

Makes 3 cups powdered mix, enough for 24 servings

CHAPTER FIVE

HOW TO HAVE A FAR-OUT SÉANCE PARTY

CALLING ALL SOULS:

I f you happen to be sitting in Serendipity on a Wednesday around two or three in the afternoon and you listen very quietly, you just might hear Marilyn Monroe sobbing. You see, this was the hour she would always stop in after her acting class at Lee Strasberg's famous Actors Studio in 1955. We don't know whether she's crying because she can't get her favorite lemon ice-box pie in heaven or because she still can't get her lines down for *How to Marry a Millionaire*. But her spirit lingers, alongside many other members of our famous and infamous clientele from the past fifty years who have moved on.

On occasion, Serendipity holds a séance to bring back long-lost friends for one last Frrrozen Hot Chocolate. After all, parties are about reaching out to friends . . . dead or alive. Marilyn is an excellent choice, as she allegedly died with a phone in her hand. Choosing a particular celebrity (or friend) with whom you'd like to communicate helps focus the party. Plan ahead with a moon calendar and try to align your party with a full moon, or better yet, pick a night with a blue moon (when there are two full moons in one month). There's nothing like a full moon to make the spirits sing, werewolves howl, and Warhol call.

PARTY MENU

VEGETABLE DIP

DON'T SELL YOUR SOUL TO THE
DEVILED EGGS (page 68)

TAKE A WALK ON THE DARK SIDE
BLACK BEAN CHILI (page 69)

SPIRITED CORN BREAD
(page 70)

CLAIRVOYANT COOKIES
(page 71)

POACHED PEARS

VISIONS OF WARHOL

In 1996 we decided to try to make contact with our old friend Andy Warhol. The illustrious medium John Edward agreed to preside over our séance. Because spirits are more likely to visit with people they know, a handful of Andy's friends gathered to help contact him. Edward received the first vibe from someone whose name he said started with a "J" and who had a connection to the Hamptons. The assembled group deduced it was Jed Johnson, a one-time intimate of Warhol's. Edward continued: "He [Jed] is with someone who's like a mother or brother figure to him. A blond. With a name that starts with A-N." Taylor Mead, who played the starring role in Andy's *Tarzan*, puffed out his Tarzan chest and blurted out: "That's Andy!"

IT'S ALL IN THE CARDS

"I see you" is a classic and slightly creepy message from the beyond, and it's also the perfect way to start a serendipitous invitation to your far-out séance. To create suggestively occult invitations, find a set of ornate tarot cards and a bunch of blank cards in rich jewel tones, such as the sapphire blue shown, that are slightly larger than the tarot cards. Center one tarot card (don't send your friend the death card!) on the front of the invitation with double-sided tape (you might use removable tape to allow your guests to keep their cards). Match certain cards such as The Magician, The Moon, or The Lovers to certain guests—you know your friends best. Use a gold or silver pen to inscribe the invitation with celestially inspired details, such as in what phase of the moon your party will occur.

HOW TO INSTANT MESSAGE YOUR DFFs (DEADEST FRIENDS FOREVER)

✳ Do not turn on your computer. In fact, turn it off, along with your cell phone, television, Game Boy, Xbox 360, and all other electronic devices. The dead are not impressed by new technology.

✳ Start by finding the right space for haunting. And we're not talking about your favorite dive bar, even if it is filled with the undead. Attics, basements, and rooms with eaves all lend the necessary claustrophobic creepiness.

✳ Clear out a large space in the middle of the room. Either use a table (round preferably), or spread a blanket or cloth on the floor. If you're contacting someone you knew personally, put something of theirs (anything from pocket lint to a favorite handkerchief) on the table or blanket.

✳ Set the ghostly mood with candlelight and incense—votives, tapered candles, or anything that won't generate too much light. Before lighting the candles, make sure that they are stable and not too close to anything flammable. Make the room as dark as possible by turning out all the overhead and other electric lights and closing the curtains.

✳ Place a Ouija board on the table or blanket with a flourish. If you don't have a Ouija board, a crystal ball will do just fine. Have neither? Then everyone must hold hands and ask for a sign.

✳ If there is no professional medium in attendance, choose someone in the group to act as a medium or allow everyone to take turns. The most spiritually minded person may have the most success (i.e., the one with New Age crystals, not the buyer for Bergdorf).

✳ For a summoning in which the whole group participates, everyone places two fingers on the Ouija indicator (or they hold hands) and asks for a sign.

✳ Listen and watch carefully, as anything may be a sign: wind blowing, cars honking, a cricket chirping, a candle going out, lights going on, rain falling, rent paid on time.

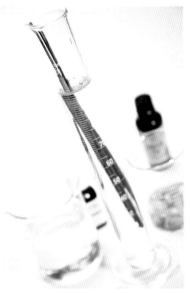

BEYOND PATCHOULI AND SANDALWOOD

Incense can be made from any fragrance oil that's used to make candles or soap. Experiment by combining some of your favorite scents in tiny amounts.

To prevent excessive smoking, fragrance oil should be mixed with a cutting agent like DPG (dipropylene glycol). DPG can be purchased online and at certain pharmacies, chemical supply stores, and janitorial supply stores. Never use alcohol as a cutting agent.

INGREDIENTS

• DPG

• Unscented incense sticks or cones (also called bamboo diffusers)

• Glass measuring cup

• Glass dish or tall vase

• Tray and paper towels

Mix 2 parts DPG with 1 part fragrance oil. Soak the incense cones or sticks in the diluted oil in a glass dish or vase. Incense sticks should be covered at least until the entire "punk" (burning end) is submerged. Cover and let them soak for 24 hours or up to 3 days.

Remove the sticks or cones from the fragrance oil. The leftover fragrance mixture can be used again for future batches. Lay the soaked incense on a breathable surface to dry (a window screen or wire rack covered with paper towels or newspaper is ideal) for at least 48 hours. You can set a fan near the incense to speed the drying process (making sure that it does not blow away the incense). You might also lay the soaked incense in sunlight to dry it more quickly, but definitely do not dry the incense in your oven, as that will not work and is dangerous.

Once the incense has dried thoroughly, it is ready to be packaged, burned, or stored. For long-term storage, keep your incense in a plastic bag or covered container to prevent the scent from fading.

HOMEMADE DECOUPAGE OUIJA BOARD

Decoupage is a simple, centuries-old technique of adorning objects and furniture with decorative paper and images—basically wallpapering stuff other than walls. With a Ouija board, you must arrange letters and numbers according to a traditional pattern, but you can otherwise be as wildly creative as you'd like. Decoupage requires relatively few specialty supplies: glue or paper adhesive (Royal Coat or Mod Podge are recommended), a brush or brushes for applying the glue, and a brayer or straightedge or ideally a bone folder (a polished tool made of bone) for smoothing the glued paper.

1. Find an old framed map, a serving tray, a used game board, an odd framed picture or other rectangular-shaped object that you don't mind covering up. The ideal size is about 15 by 20 inches and at least 1/4 inch thick. For a lighterweight Ouija, you can use heavy craft board (available at art supply stores) that can easily be cut to any size.

2. Choose a thematic background for your Ouija board, such as a large sheet of decorative wrapping or art paper, or a map. Lightly dilute your glue with a little water, and brush the glue in a thin, even coat over your entire board. Carefully center your background on the board and use the brayer or straightedge to smooth out any bubbles or creases, starting from the center and moving to the outer edges. Let the glue dry while you assemble the letters, numbers, and images for your board.

3. The basic Ouija board design starts with "Yes" in the upper left corner, "No" in the upper right corner, the alphabet in the center divided into two equal rows of letters, the numbers 0 through 9

under the alphabet, and finally a "Good-Bye" in the bottom center. Aside from these required elements, feel free to decorate the edges as you wish with astrological symbols, drawings, snapshots, or pictures cut from books or magazines. Go to town embellishing the board, but remember that you want to maintain a smooth surface. Brush the underside of your cutouts with the lightly diluted glue and carefully apply to the board.

4. Once your board's design is complete, coat the wood or glass or canvas with clear lacquer, enamel, or polyurethane (found at craft or hardware stores) to create a smooth, slick surface, ensuring that the planchette will glide easily.

5. Make or find something appropriate to use as a planchette. It can be made of wood, clear plastic, or any other lightweight material. If you want to get fancy, cut a hole in the planchette large enough to see a letter through it. Put felt pads on the bottom, so it glides smoothly over the board. If you're not in the mood to make a planchette, defer to the tradition of using a wineglass, teacup, lucky coin, or antique pocket watch as a message indicator.

ROCKING THE DEAD

1. "No-One But You," Queen
2. "Over the Rainbow," Judy Garland
3. "The Sounds of Silence," Simon & Garfunkel
4. "Walking with a Ghost," Tegan and Sara
5. "Stairway to Heaven," Led Zeppelin
6. "I'll Follow You into the Dark," Death Cab for Cutie
7. "Everybody Hurts," R.E.M.
8. "Hide and Seek," Imogen Heap
9. "The Man Who Sold the World," Nirvana
10. "Such Great Heights," The Postal Service
11. "Grace," Kate Havnevik
12. "Highway to Hell," AC/DC
13. "Let Go," Frou Frou

DON'T SELL YOUR SOUL TO THE DEVILED EGGS

6 large eggs

1/2 cup sun-dried tomatoes (not packed in oil)

2 tablespoons minced fresh chives

1/8 teaspoon cayenne pepper

2 to 3 tablespoons mayonnaise

1 teaspoon white wine vinegar

1 teaspoon Dijon mustard

Salt and pepper

Paprika

To hard-boil the eggs, pierce each one with a needle to prevent them from cracking. Fill a large saucepan with enough water to cover the eggs, and bring it to a boil over high heat. Reduce the heat and simmer for 10 minutes. Remove the eggs from the saucepan and immediately submerge them in cold water. When the eggs have cooled, carefully peel them.

Cut the eggs lengthwise in half. Over a medium bowl, gently squeeze the egg halves, and the cooked yolks should pop out into the bowl. Mash the yolks coarsely with a fork. Finely chop 2 of the egg white halves and blend into the yolks. Finely chop 1/4 cup of the sun-dried tomatoes. Add the chopped sun-dried tomatoes, chives, cayenne pepper, mayonnaise, vinegar, and mustard; mix well. Season with salt and pepper. Spoon about 1 tablespoon of the yolk mixture into each egg white half, mounding slightly. Sprinkle with paprika. For a devilish garnish, make sun-dried tomato horns by cutting the remaining 1/4 cup sun-dried tomatoes into 3/4-inch-long strips and placing 2 strips in each egg, pushing them 1/4 of the way into the filling to secure.

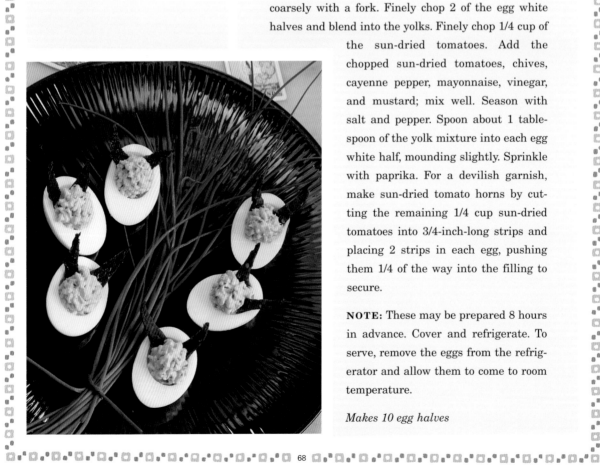

NOTE: These may be prepared 8 hours in advance. Cover and refrigerate. To serve, remove the eggs from the refrigerator and allow them to come to room temperature.

Makes 10 egg halves

TAKE A WALK ON THE DARK SIDE BLACK BEAN CHILI

1 to 2 tablespoons olive oil

2 pounds ground beef, chicken, or turkey

1 large onion, diced

1 1/2 tablespoons minced garlic

3/4 cup dark beer

1 (28-ounce) can whole crushed peeled tomatoes, pureed

1/4 cup ancho chili powder

1 tablespoon ground cumin

1 1/4 cups chicken stock

2 (16-ounce) cans black beans, rinsed and drained

3 tablespoons fresh lime juice

Salt and freshly ground black pepper

3/4 cup chopped cilantro

Sour cream (optional)

Grated Cheddar cheese (optional)

In a large frying pan over medium-high heat, heat the oil almost to smoking. Sauté the ground meat until browned, about 10 minutes. Add the onion and garlic and cook for 3 minutes, but do not allow them to burn. Add the beer and cook until the liquid has completely evaporated. Reduce the heat to a simmer. Add the tomatoes, chili powder, and cumin. Stir well and cook for 10 minutes.

Pour in the stock and simmer for 40 minutes. Add the beans and simmer for 15 minutes. Degrease the pan if necessary. Stir in the lime juice and salt and pepper to taste. Transfer the chili to a serving dish and garnish with the cilantro. Serve with sour cream and grated Cheddar cheese, if desired.

Makes 10 servings

SPIRITED CORN BREAD

2 cups yellow cornmeal

2 cups all-purpose flour

1 1/2 teaspoons salt

2 teaspoons baking powder

1 teaspoon baking soda

2 eggs, lightly beaten

3/4 cup honey

2 cups buttermilk

8 tablespoons (1 stick) unsalted butter, melted, plus more for the skillet

2 cups creamed corn or fresh corn kernels

3 canned chipotle chilis, pureed (optional)

1 jalapeño pepper, seeds and stems removed, finely minced

Preheat the oven to 450 degrees F. Preheat a 12-inch cast-iron skillet in the oven for 20 minutes.

In a large mixing bowl, combine the cornmeal, flour, salt, baking powder, and baking soda. Fold in the eggs, honey, buttermilk, butter, corn, chipotles (if using), and jalapeño.

Brush the preheated skillet with melted butter and immediately pour in the batter (it should reach approximately three-fourths of the way up). Be careful not to touch the pan, as it will be extremely hot. Bake for 15 to 20 minutes, or until the corn bread is brown around the edges and firm.

NOTE: If you don't have a cast-iron skillet, you can bake at 375 degrees F for 15 minutes in 2 muffin tins. You need not preheat the tin, but you do need to grease or line it with paper or foil muffin cups before adding the batter.

Makes 1 large corn bread or 24 corn muffins

CLAIRVOYANT COOKIES

2 cups rolled oats

1 cup brown sugar

1/4 teaspoon salt

2 teaspoons baking powder

8 tablespoons (1 stick) unsalted butter, melted

1 egg, beaten

3/4 cup mini chocolate chips (optional)

In a large mixing bowl, combine the oats, sugar, salt, and baking powder. Stir in the melted butter. Add the egg and mix well. Add the chocolate chips, if desired. Refrigerate the dough for 15 minutes. While the dough is chilling, preheat the oven to 350 degrees F, and grease one or more cookie sheets or line with parchment paper. When ready to bake, shape the dough into 1/2-inch-round balls and place them 1 inch apart on the prepared cookie sheets. Bake for 8 to 10 minutes, until lightly browned around the edges. Let the cookies stand for 1 minute before removing from the pan to a cooling rack.

NOTE: These cookies freeze well and taste good even when they are frozen.

Makes between 5 and 6 dozen

CHAPTER SIX

HOW TO AVOID A DOUR SHOWER

PRENUPTIAL GAMES:

We've accommodated many a gentleman who has been inspired to drop a ring into his lady's Frrrozen Hot Chocolate before dropping to his knees to pop the big question. These days our reservationist often hears, "But I must get a table tonight, I'm getting engaged." It wasn't easy creating an atmosphere of Victorian romance hip enough for Warhol and friends. In the early years, Patch, Calvin, and I used to hop aboard the El train (the elevated train before the subway), head for the Bowery, and scour the city for funky tableware, interesting tchotchkes, historical memorabilia, and unusual white china.

There are lots of ways, however, to replicate Serendipity's funky elegance in your home. Splash touches of bold color amidst an otherwise all-white decor. Set an all-white table, but use giant fake rings with different color "gems" as napkin holders. Ask your guests to come dressed in white, but let the bride-to-be stand out in red or black or whatever color she chooses. Maybe she'll want to go punk with purple hair!

At Serendipity, we revel in mixing the traditional with the untraditional. If the bride likes the idea of having the men attend, don't be a slave to an all-female bridal shower. Start the couple on their marital journey by promoting the idea that the household domain is both the man's and the woman's responsibility. Instead of a fussy ladies' luncheon, throw a casual coed barbecue. Party games such as The Newlywed Game or Dress Rehearsal can be much more fun when men are included. Rather than having guests bring typical household item gifts, come up with a theme to direct their gift giving, such as "Stock the Bar" or "Bring on the Barbecue."

PARTY MENU

VEGETABLE CHIPS

WATERMELON FRUIT BOWL
(page 78)

CRAB CAKES

ASPARAGUS VICHYSSOISE
(page 79)

PASSIONATE PAVLOVA
EXTRAVAGANZA
(page 80)

SPARKLING PEACH SANGRIA
(page 81)

WELCOME IN WHITE

Find a space in your home that would fit a cozy canopy, such as a front hall, a small entryway, or an outdoor gazebo. Create a wedding canopy with rolls of 1-inch white crepe paper. Tape the midpoint of a long piece of crepe paper to the ceiling in the middle of an entryway. Tack or tape the same piece again at the two points where the ceiling meets the wall, and let the ends cascade to the floor. Cover the entire ceiling of the entryway in this manner, spacing the strips of crepe paper about 2 inches apart, and trimming the ends to the same length, creating a long arch.

LOVE LIGHTS THE WAY

For an evening shower, homemade luminaries can brighten the path to your house or apartment.

Purchase about two dozen white paper lunch bags.

Cut one 3-inch heart-shaped hole on each side of every paper bag.

Fill each bag with gravel, sand (available at plant stores or the beach), or potting soil to weight the luminary.

Secure one votive candle inside each bag.

Line the path to your door (or the length of your front hall) with the luminaries and light them just before the shower begins. (Don't forget to blow out the flames at the end of the party.)

SOUND THE WEDDING BELLS

1. "You Made Me Love You," Judy Garland
2. "I Get a Kick Out of You," Frank Sinatra
3. "Earth Angel," The Penguins
4. "Caring Is Creepy," The Shins
5. "I Can't Help Falling in Love with You," Elvis Presley
6. "I Only Have Eyes for You," The Flamingos
7. "I Don't Know Why" AKA "Don't Know Why I Love You," The Rolling Stones
8. "Sweet Caroline," Neil Diamond
9. "Love of My Life," Queen
10. "The Things We Do for Love," 10 cc

LOOKING INTO THE FUTURE

Remember those paper fortune-tellers that kept your friends so engrossed in grade school? You would write answers such as "Yes," "No," and "Ask Again" on a piece of paper, fold it in a special way, and then invite people to ask questions. The folded-up fortune-teller would reveal answers to pressing questions like "Will Jimmy ask me out?" just like a magical eight ball. Well, a bridal shower is a perfect time to regress into adolescent patterns and share some girly gossip. How about making fortune-tellers (like those shown) to draw out your guests and catch a glimpse into the future? Instead of "Yes" and "No" answers, compile random, funny tidbits to write under the flaps—such as the names of possible suitors or things the bride might say—or do—on her wedding night. One guest opens and closes the fortune-teller while other guests ask questions and select the flaps to open for revealing answers.

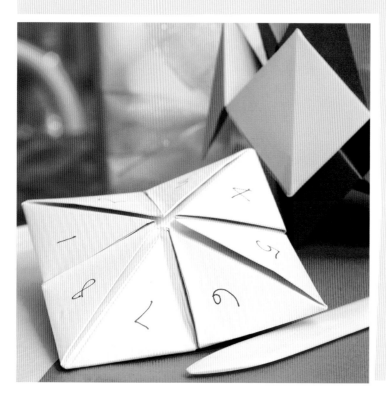

A GIFT FOR EVERY HOUR

The bridal shower got its start with people coming together to help poor women who lacked a dowry by "showering" them with gifts. When you throw a shower shindig, keep in mind, regardless of the engaged couple's economic situation, it's an opportunity to help them begin a new life together. The goal is to provide the newlyweds with what they will enjoy and may need as they venture into matrimony. And to prevent guests from showering the newlyweds with too many waffle irons, consider giving an "Hours of the Day" party.

Feature a large clock on the invitation that pairs each guest with a particular hour. One card might read, "It's 6:00 in the morning, help our bride get out of bed," and another could say, "It's midnight, what is the bride to wear?" Whoever is assigned 6 AM might bring a coffee maker, and

the person covering midnight could purchase sexy lingerie for the bride-to-be. Always remember to take into account the couple's interests and tastes. If the bride or groom is an avid cook, appropriate gifts might be an omelet pan for a morning hour and a soufflé dish for nighttime.

AND THE BRIDE WORE . . . PAPER

Divide the party into teams of two. At a coed shower, couples can be teams. One member of each team is the "bride model" and the other is the "designer." Each team is given one roll of toilet paper, from which it must design a wedding dress (train and veil optional) on the model. No glue, tape, or scissors allowed. Decide on how much time (fifteen minutes

perhaps) to allow for completing the task. Everyone starts at the same time. If you want to provide privacy for the teams, assign separate rooms in which to design their creations. When time's up, the toilet paper–clad models must walk the runway to be judged by the other competitors (you can't vote for your own team) who will pick the best gown.

It has been said that picking out a watermelon is like picking out a wife. You can look at it, turn it around, squeeze it, and thump it, but you never know enough about it until it's too late! If you've picked a not-too-sweet watermelon, it is possible to improve on nature's work—just add sugar. And here's a particularly pretty way to serve your juicy, sweet watermelon:

❋ Select a large round watermelon (12 to 14 pounds).

❋ Cut a thin slice of rind off the bottom lengthwise, so that the watermelon will rest securely on a flat surface.

❋ Cut one-third off the top lengthwise. Make a sawtooth pattern along the edge of the "bowl" by repeatedly cutting out side-by-side "V" shapes.

❋ Scoop out the flesh and seeds using a melon baller or cut the fruit into cubes, but leave the shell intact. Discard the seeds.

❋ Dissolve 4 (3-ounce) packages of watermelon flavor (or other flavor) Jell-O in 4 cups of boiling water in a large bowl. Once the Jell-O has dissolved completely, stir in 4 cups of cold water. Refrigerate until the gelatin has thickened slightly, and stir in half of the reserved fruit.

❋ Spoon the Jell-O mixture into the watermelon bowl.

❋ Top with the remaining balls or cubes of watermelon. To add color, you can mix the watermelon pieces with honeydew or cantaloupe melon, cut into balls or cubes as well. Refrigerate until ready to serve.

ASPARAGUS VICHYSSOISE

3 tablespoons unsalted butter

1 medium onion, diced, or 2 medium leeks, white parts only, cleaned and chopped

1 large russet potato, peeled and diced

3 pounds asparagus

3 cups chicken stock

Salt and pepper

1 1/2 cups heavy cream

16 cherry tomatoes, chopped (optional)

Add the butter to a large skillet and place over medium heat. Add the onion or leeks to the skillet and sauté until soft but not browned. Add the diced potato and continue cooking until it softens but does not brown.

Snap off and discard the tough ends of the asparagus spears. Cut off the tender tips, about 1 to 1 1/2 inches long, and reserve the stems. Bring a large pot of salted water to a boil and drop in the asparagus tips, cooking until just tender, about 1 minute. Plunge the tips into cold water to stop them from cooking. Drain the tips and pat dry. Slice the reserved asparagus stems into 1-inch pieces.

Add the chicken stock to the onion and potato mixture and bring to a boil. Add the sliced asparagus stems. Bring to a boil and cook for 10 minutes. Season with salt and pepper. Add the cream and simmer for an additional 15 minutes. In a blender, puree the onion and potato mixture and pass it through a mesh strainer. Serve the soup hot or cold, garnished with the reserved asparagus tips and cherry tomatoes (if desired).

Makes 8 servings

PASSIONATE PAVLOVA EXTRAVAGANZA

9 egg whites, at room temperature

2 1/2 cups superfine sugar

3 teaspoons distilled white vinegar

5 teaspoons vanilla extract

2 tablespoons cornstarch

3 cups heavy cream

1 cup confectioners' sugar

3 pints fresh fruit (a mix of any of the following: strawberries, blueberries, raspberries, kiwi, passion fruit, pomegranate seeds; large pieces cut into 1/4-inch cubes)

Preheat the oven to 300 degrees F.

In a large mixing bowl, beat the egg whites with an electric mixer until soft peaks form. Add 1/2 cup of cold water and beat again. While still beating, gradually add the superfine sugar, vinegar, and 3 teaspoons of the vanilla. Reduce speed and sift in the cornstarch.

Line a cookie sheet with a large piece of waxed paper or parchment paper and butter the paper. Pile the meringue into a large round mound. Use a spoon to create a well that measures 3 to 5 inches in diameter inside a 2-inch-thick wall of meringue. Then, bake the pavlova for 45 minutes. Turn off the oven and let the meringue cool in the oven. Do not open the oven door. When cool, remove the cookie sheet from the oven and gently slide the pavlova shell onto a decorative serving plate.

To make the whipped cream, beat the cream until soft peaks begin to form. Add the confectioners' sugar and the remaining 2 teaspoons of vanilla and beat again to soft peaks. Fill the well of the pavlova with the whipped cream and top with the fruit.

NOTE: Sometimes (depending on weather or a number of other factors) the pavlova can start to crack. Do not despair! Simply spread over the cracks with more whipped cream.

Makes 10 to 12 servings

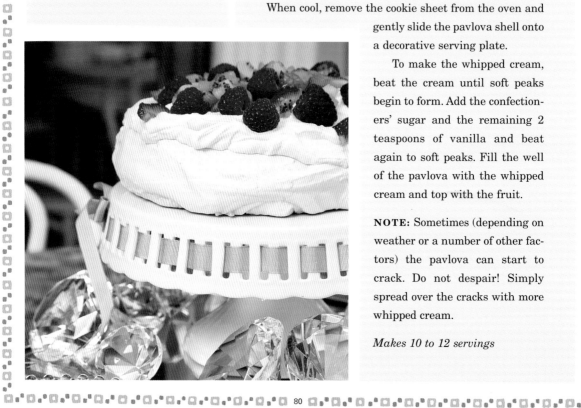

SPARKLING
PEACH SANGRIA

4 firm ripe peaches, cut into 1/4-inch wedges

2/3 cup superfine sugar

1 cup peach schnapps

2 quarts (or liters) chilled rosé or white Zinfandel wine

4 cups chilled sparkling water

Combine the peaches and sugar in a large pitcher and let it sit until the sugar has dissolved and the fruit is macerated (softened from steeping in the liquid). Add the schnapps, wine, sparkling water, and enough ice to fill the pitcher halfway. Serve immediately.

VARIATION: For a nonalcoholic version, replace the schnapps and wine with 2 quarts of ginger ale.

Makes about 10 servings

CHAPTER SEVEN

BREEZY SUMMER SOIREES:

ICE CREAM DREAMS

When the summer heat would crank up, and New Yorkers looked like they were beginning to melt, Serendipity used to give away ice cream on the street. Although that tradition is no more, we are still the place in town for ice cream whether it's Katie Holmes and her little girl, Suri, eating a Can't Say No Sundae; a pregnant Sofia Coppola downing a Forbidden Broadway Sundae; or David Copperfield making his sundae disappear.

Ice cream goes hand in hand with summer parties. And what a perfect way to kick off the warm weather season by having a lawn party, tailgate party, terrace party, or picnic in the park. The one requirement is that it must take place outside, and the one rule is: Don't forget the ice cream. Or the hot dogs. Or the hamburgers. But regardless of what's on the menu, it's the spirit of the gathering that matters most. After all, "picnic" comes from the French word *pique-nique*, which means to pick at things of little importance.

For some, the main concern is not what's being served, but what it's being served on. The famed Broadway and film diva Carol Channing once showed up at Serendipity for Anita Loos's birthday party carrying her own elegant picnic hamper. Our staff suppressed more than a few giggles as she pulled out silver dishes and flatware. Apparently she was on a special diet that meant she could only eat off of silver!

PARTY MENU

SUMMER BRIESBURGER
(page 89)

FOOT-LONG HOT DOGS

POTATO CHIPS

AN ASSORTMENT OF
ICE CREAMS

A RAINBOW OF ICICLES
(page 90)

FROZEN CHOCOLATE-DIPPED
BANANAS

PIMM'S CUP
(page 91)

SWAYING TO SUMMER

1. "A Hard Day's Night," The Beatles
2. "Love Is Strange," Mickey and Sylvia
3. "Yes, Indeed," Tommy Dorsey
4. "Summer in the City," Regina Spektor
5. "Que Sera, Sera (Whatever Will Be, Will Be)," Doris Day
6. "April Come She Will," Art Garfunkel
7. "You Are My Sunshine," Norman Blake
8. "Into the Sun," Robert Gomez
9. "Peaceful Easy Feeling," The Eagles
10. "Do You Wanna Dance?" The Beach Boys
11. "It's Everything But Party Time," The Go-Go's
12. "Imitation of Life," R.E.M.
13. "I Am a Rock," Simon & Garfunkel

A SUNDAE BAR

If you have no yard but yearn for a summer party, throw an ice cream social. Decorate your home like a 1950s ice cream parlor. If you have an island in your kitchen, set stools around it like an old-time soda fountain. Set the table with old-fashioned bottles of seltzer, a blender for milkshakes, and cones wrapped in paper doilies. Choose several flavors of ice cream and nestle the pints into a large bowl filled with ice. For the whipped cream, buy a pressurized canister so folks can top their sundaes like a professional. Use a Crock-Pot or fondue pot to keep hot fudge and caramel sauces warm. Have lots of little bowls filled with different toppings and mix-ins. Rent an old-style popcorn maker. Hire a barbershop quartet. Make sure the men are wearing vests, mustaches, straw hats, and arm garters. The women can sport frilly hats, parasols, and lace fans.

JUICY INVITES

When designing the invitations for your party, look for inspiration from that most delicious summertime treat—watermelon.

Fold an 8.5 x 11-inch sheet of paper or card stock in half lengthwise and then in half again widthwise. Trim and round off the outer corners to create an oblong shape, like a watermelon, about 7 inches long.

Print your invitation text vertically down the center of a regular 8.5 x 11-inch sheet of hot pink stationery in a splashy font, making sure that the entire text will fit on the oblong template. Place the oblong template on the pink paper, trace around it, and cut out the watermelon-shaped invitation.

Glue the pink oblong onto a sheet of white stationery. Trim around the oblong, leaving a slim border of white.

Center the white-bordered invitation over an 8.5 x 11-inch sheet of bright green stationery or heavy card stock. Trim out the oblong again, leaving a thinner border of bright green.

Trace the bright green oblong on a sheet of lighter green stationery and cut out wavy lines to fit the curve of the melon shape. Glue these to the outside of the green oblong to resemble a watermelon's stripes.

Use a sheet of black paper to cut out small, rounded seed shapes. Glue these along the outer edge of the pink paper at the center of the invitation to resemble watermelon seeds. This tiny touch is surprisingly convincing.

Using a bone folder or other straightedge, make a single clean crease across the center of the invitation, if necessary, to fit it into an envelope.

WICKED WICKETS

We appreciate the Victorian sense of discretion—the way life was lived with so much bubbling just beneath the surface. With so much that's in your face about pop culture today, it is refreshing, even exciting, to hearken back to a time when subtlety was cultivated. Croquet was an especially popular leisure-time activity for women in the 1850s, as it was a new experience for women to be able to play an outdoor game in the company of men. In Victorian England, games were carefully chaperoned. Tight croquet, the practice of putting a foot on one ball and sending the opponent's ball flying into the bushes, allowed young men to disappear with young women into the bushes to search for the ball. By the 1860s, garden parties began to be called croquet parties.

To host this lawn game, ask your guests to come dressed all in white. Buy or borrow the necessary equipment (pictured, clockwise from top right, are balls, mallets, wickets, and posts). Learn the rules and set up the course in advance of the party. There are several configurations for arranging croquet wickets, but the most popular is a double diamond, consisting of two diamonds stacked on top of each other (like a figure eight). The object of the game is to move your ball through as many wickets as possible. Assign your guests to teams so the greatest number of people can play at once, and bestow trophies on members of the winning team.

aBUNdance

Hot dogs are a New York tradition. One of the earliest print mentions of them was in 1906 when a newspaper cartoonist recorded the sale of hot dogs during a New York Giants baseball game at the Polo Grounds (155th Street and Eighth Avenue). It was not, as legend had it, the first mention in print of "hot dog," which occurred in 1893. Like New York City, Serendipity is always ready to take a tradition and exaggerate it. We stretched the Big Apple's appetite by popularizing the foot-long hot dog in the early 1960s. We used to serve them with a twelve-inch ruler until too many of the plastic "feet" began walking out the door. But the foot-long has remained one of our greatest attractions. When Monica Lewinsky came to the restaurant to celebrate her thirty-first birthday, she ordered the foot-long. When the waiter placed the dish in front of her, she gasped, "Oh, my God!" When Beyoncé visited recently, she requested that hers be served with chili—much to the amusement of her boyfriend Jay-Z. When making these grand dogs for a party, be sure to accompany them with an array of decadent toppings so guests can satisfy their favorite tastes or experiment with new combinations. Here's a starter set of toppings: chopped onion, crumbled bacon, grated Cheddar cheese, chili, pickle relish, and cole slaw. Allow yourself to get extravagant—guacamole, anyone?—and don't forget to offer several different types of mustard. Considering the dogs' awesome size, you might want to serve them on oversized platters like we do.

BEACH BLANKET BINGO

A summer shower can come at the most inopportune hour. So if you're planning an outdoor party, always have a backup plan. For example, you can collect a bunch of colorful beach blankets (one for each guest), and arrange them in a large cleared-out area in your living room. Then bring the party inside. You can assign each person to a particular blanket. For entertainment, pull out a bingo set. After each round, everyone switches blankets, like musical chairs. To add to the beachy atmosphere, make miniature coolers and place them around the room. Buy a bunch of neon-colored plastic sand pails. Fill each with ice, and stash a few bottles of your favorite brew inside. Guests won't need to get up for refills, and everyone will love not getting sand in their drinks.

SUMMER BRIESBURGER

1 egg

1/3 cup chopped onion

1/3 cup chopped parsley

1 1/4 teaspoons salt

1/2 teaspoon freshly ground pepper

2 pounds ground beef

20 cubes (1/2 inch each) Brie cheese (or Port Salut or Gruyère)

1/2 cup to 1 cup bread crumbs

2 tablespoons unsalted butter

20 mini brioche buns

In a blender or food processor, puree the egg, onion, and parsley. Add the salt and pepper. Spoon the mixture into a large mixing bowl and stir in the beef. Divide the mixture into 20 1/2-inch-thick patties. Poke a cube of cheese into the center of each patty, using your fingers to cover the cheese completely with the meat. Dredge each patty in bread crumbs. Melt the butter in a large, heavy skillet over medium-high heat, and cook the patties for about 5 minutes per side. Cook in batches if necessary. . Cook long enough so that the cheese in the middle is completely melted. You can test by sticking a toothpick into the center, and if it comes out gooey, the cheese is melted. Toast the buns if desired in a toaster oven or in an oven set at 400 degrees F for 5 minutes, or until golden.

NOTE: The burgers can also be grilled.

Makes 20 mini burgers

A RAINBOW OF ICICLES

WONDERFUL WATERMELON

4 cups watermelon, seeds removed, coarsely chopped

10 mint leaves (optional)

CHERRY GOOD POPS

2 cups pitted cherries

1/2 cup sugar

1 cup plain yogurt

PIÑA COLADA

2 cups crushed canned pineapple with liquid, or 2 cups chopped fresh pineapple

1 cup shredded sweetened coconut

DREAMY CREAMY

1 (6-ounce) can frozen orange juice concentrate

6 ounces water

1 pint vanilla ice cream, softened, or plain yogurt

Making homemade frozen pops is so easy—and the result is a treat that's fruity, refreshing, and good for you. Finding the sticks, however, can sometimes be difficult, so plan ahead and buy a bunch at the supermarket or order them online at americanwood crafterssupply.com or another online source. The basic recipe below shows you how to make any frozen pop, including the four flavor variations we've suggested. Simply combine all the ingredients listed for the flavored pops, and follow the instructions outlined in the basic recipe.

BASIC RECIPE

Combine all the ingredients in a blender or food processor, and puree until smooth. Pour the mixture into small 4-ounce paper cups or pop molds and freeze. Insert the wooden sticks after 2 hours, or when the mixture begins to thicken and get slushy. Return the pops to the freezer and allow them to harden, approximately 4 hours depending on the freezer temperature.

Makes about 8 (2 1/2-ounce) icicles

PIMM'S CUP

1 shot Pimm's gin

8 ounces 7-Up (or other lemon-lime soda)

1 slice each lemon, orange, and tart apple

1 slice cucumber, 5 to 6 inches long, cut lengthwise

2 large mint leaves, slightly crushed

Pour a shot of Pimm's gin into a highball glass filled with ice. Add the 7-Up or lemon-lime soda. Garnish with the fruit slices, cucumber, and mint leaves.

Kid-Friendly Variation: For a sparkling lemonade drink that kids will love, omit the shot of Pimm's gin.

Makes 1 serving

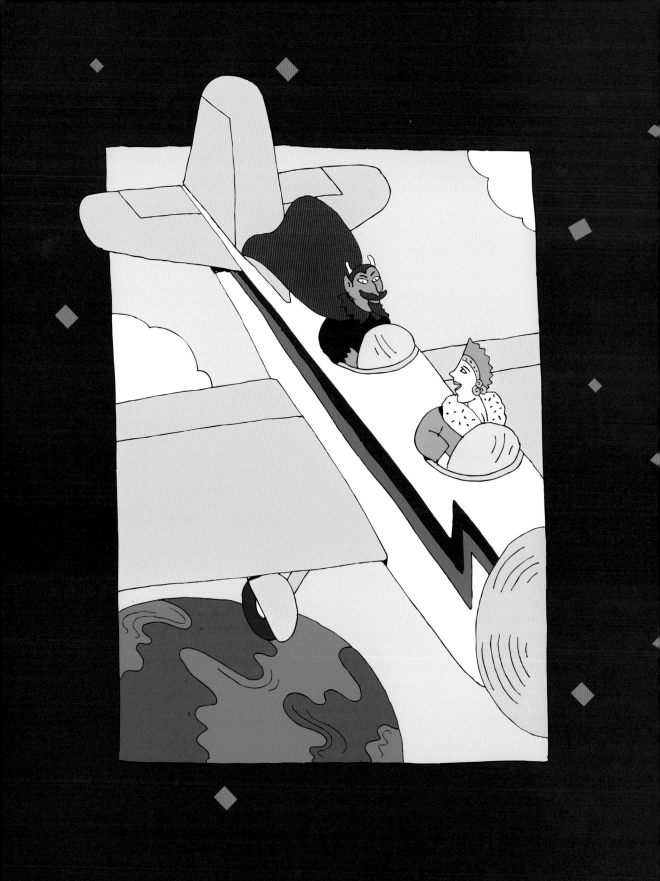

CHAPTER EIGHT

A MOVEABLE FEAST:

CRUISIN' THE CONTINENTS FROM YOUR BARCALOUNGER

Sometimes Serendipity seems more like the United Nations than a restaurant. For instance, in a single week, Bill and Chelsea Clinton, Panama's President Martin Torrijos, and Princesses Eugenia and Beatrice from England all converged serendipitously to sample our sweets. We've become a destination for tourists from all over the globe, and since the romantic comedy *Serendipity* came out in 2001, many tourists have traveled halfway around the world to sip Frrrozen Hot Chocolates, insisting on sitting upstairs where the movie was filmed!

Even if you can't book the best cabin on the *QEII* or fly off to Bermuda at the drop of a hat, you can take your friends on a culinary safari without leaving home. Star chef Rachael Ray, who travels the world for new flavors, visited us recently and said the key to expanding your gustatory horizons is not being afraid to try new things.

Planning a party is not unlike getting ready for a trip—you make to-do lists, decide on your meals and wardrobe, and pick the right dates on the calendar. In our early days in New York, our circle of friends consisted of out-of-work actors, fashion designers, and artists, so we had no money for fancy vacations. Instead, we draped saris, hung piñatas, and ordered Chinese food. Highlighting the flavors, fabrics, and accents from far-off lands can take you miles away without making you set foot outside your own living room. From chocolate tastings to an armchair tour of Spain, here are plenty of ideas to send you cruising in style.

Party Menu

WASABI BAR NUTS
(page 100)

TANDOORI DRUMSTICKS
(page 101)

THAI SLAW
(page 102)

SELECTION OF BITTERSWEET
CHOCOLATES

CANDY SUSHI
(page 103)

BLOOD ORANGE SLICES WITH
ORANGE FLOWER WATER

SELECTION OF INDIA PALE ALES

JET-SET INVITATIONS

What says "Take me away" better than a luggage tag? Many stationery and art stores sell sets of blank cards styled like luggage tags (as shown), but punching a hole and snipping two corners off a piece of card stock is a do-it-yourself way to accomplish the same look. Print up the information for your party on separate paper with dates, times, and locations in a glamorous script reminiscent of the Golden Age of Travel. Decorate the outside of the envelopes with stickers (or reproductions) from exotic hotels, tropical ports of call, or international airlines (found at some art supply/stationery/card shops and in some clip art books) to give your guests the impression that the invitations have circled the globe enroute to their door.

ON BOARD THE MARRAKECH EXPRESS

❋ Create a desert oasis tent in your living room or dining room. Simply fasten lengths of exotic fabric to the center of the ceiling, drape it out to the walls, and allow it to cascade to the floor. Secure any loose ends by placing them under decorative rocks or planters. Be sure to keep any open-flame candles at a safe distance from the fabric.

❋ Scatter rose petals or chocolate coins over the dining table and around the floor.

❋ Wrap a beaded wire bracelet (find these at flea markets or inexpensive jewelry stores) around a number of pillar candles and group them on terra-cotta plant saucers on a low coffee table in the center of the room. Pull together as many candle lanterns as you can and place them in attractive groupings in the corners of the room.

❋ For serving pieces, mix and match terra-cotta, majolica, and other vibrant pottery from different cultures such as Moroccan, Spanish, Japanese, and Southwestern American.

❋ Wrap several throw pillows with colorful scarves. Using two scarves for each pillow, fold each scarf into a square that will fit over the pillow. Line up the scarves so that one side of the pillow is covered with one scarf, and the second scarf covers the other side of the pillow, which is sandwiched in between the two. Tie the four corners of one scarf to the corresponding four corners of the other

scarf. (If possible, also try to tie the scarf corners to the pillow's corners.)

❋ Purchase several sets of kids' bongos for decor—and for any musically inclined guests to play.

❋ At place settings, provide small decorative bowls holding thin slices of lemon and warm water to use as finger bowls.

❋ For party favors, place an Indian beaded pill box or a miniature Buddha at each place setting.

ROCKIN' THE RIYADH

1. "Rock the Casbah," The Clash
2. "Marrakesh Express," Crosby, Stills & Nash
3. "Mexicali Blues," Grateful Dead
4. "California Dreamin'," The Mamas and The Papas
5. "The Big Country," Talking Heads
6. "Worlds Away," The Go-Go's
7. "When the World Is Running Down," The Police
8. "American Girl," Tom Petty & the Heart-breakers
9. "Born in the U.S.A.," Bruce Springsteen
10. "Australia," The Shins
11. "El Paso," Grateful Dead
12. "Don't Stand So Close to Me," The Police
13. "A Horse with No Name," America
14. "The Ocean," Led Zeppelin

MAGIC LANTERNS

1. Buy sheets of 8.5 x 11-inch card stock that have a different color on each side. Or you can glue together two sheets of different colored paper. Fold the sheets in half lengthwise and crease with a bone folder.

2. Using scissors, make five cuts along the crease, each one measuring 2 1/2 inches long, spaced 2 inches apart, and starting 2 inches from the short end of the sheet. The fifth cut will leave a strip only about an inch wide; cut out and remove this strip to leave a gap, and reserve this strip for step 4.

2. Unfold the cut sheet and bring the short sides together, so that the vertical panels bend outward at the crease. Use strong double-sided tape or glue to attach the two short tabs behind the top and bottom border of the other end. You may want to hold these together with paper clips while the glue dries.

4. Glue or tape the reserved strip to the inside of the top band to create a handle. String the lanterns evenly along a length of cord, twine, or wire, or even along a length of holiday lights for extra sparkle.

A PASSPORT STAMPED IN CHOCOLATE

When we were first developing the secret mix of chocolates to put in our famous Frrrozen Hot Chocolate, we sampled gourmet chocolate from all over the globe to be sure we had the perfect combination. What a delicious way to travel the world! Hosting an international chocolate tasting is a decadent way to achieve a truly serendipitous global perspective, and it's a surefire hit at any party.

Fine-quality chocolate is made all over the world and comes in several grades, depending on its ratio of pure cacao to other ingredients (such as sugar). When you get upwards of 70 percent cacao, the chocolate may not taste very sweet, but you can taste the other flavors and nuances. If, however, you prefer your chocolate a little sweeter and milder, opt for bittersweet chocolate, which is both complex and easily palatable. The true chocolate snob will want to sample chocolate made entirely from the beans of one plantation, called single-estate chocolate, which you can find at fine chocolatiers and gourmet markets.

You can style your chocolate tasting like a blind wine tasting, and let your guests try to guess which continent or country the chocolate comes from. Since your party is a voyage around the world, offer a mixture from far-flung, exotic regions. In our tasting, shown below, we put tiny flags on toothpicks to indicate the chocolates' countries of origin: Ecuador, Indonesia, Italy, and the United States.

Before tasting, consider the chocolate's appearance and texture. Fine chocolate should be dark and glossy, though the color can vary from a rich brown to almost black. Inhale the aroma and, just as in a wine tasting, try to identify different notes. Do you detect smoke, spice, or coffee? When tasting, allow the chocolate to melt on your tongue to release each flavor. Offer your guests cool, still water or even a light snack like tortilla chips to refresh their palates between tastings.

Treat your guests like sommeliers or critics and give each of them a small notebook and pen to record their impressions and preferences. Invite them to take home an unopened bar or small block of their favorite chocolate. It's a small—and delicious—world after all!

BYOP (BRING YOUR OWN PILLOW)

Don't be shy about borrowing things for a party. If, for instance, you want to create an interior that suggests the inside of the bottle from *I Dream of Jeannie*, and you lack the right pillows, ask your friends to help. On the invitation, ask everyone to bring a colorful pillow or two to the party. Then you can comfortably seat your guests around a low coffee table with lots of cushions and pillows.

AROUND THE WORLD IN SEVEN SITTINGS

Together with a number of friends, plan a party where you have the first course at one house or apartment and move to the next dwelling for each subsequent course. For example, start with a caipirinha in South America and move on to tandoori kebabs in Asia, lamb chops in Australia, and chocolate soufflé in Europe. Each home is assigned one of the seven continents and is responsible for serving one dish and one drink. This type of party circuit works best in a small neighborhood or urban setting where everyone can walk or travel together to the next "continent."

VIVA ESPAÑA!

Take an armchair tour around Spain with a wine and cheese potluck party. Assign each of your guests a region of the country and ask them to bring a cheese or wine that is typical of that region. Serve their offerings in small tapas dishes. Here are some ideas to get you started:

ANDALUCIA: Marcona almonds or membrillo (quince paste)
ASTURIAS: Cabrales (Spanish blue cheese)
CATALONIA: Arbequina olive oil
JEREZ: Cava (Spanish sparkling wine)
LA MANCHA: Manchego cheese
MANZANILLA: Olives
NAVARRA: Idiazabal cheese
PENEDES: Red and white wines
RIBERA DEL DUERO: Red wine
RIOJA: Red wine
RUEDA: White wine
SALAMANCA: Jamón Iberico (Spanish ham)

WASABI BAR NUTS

1 egg white

1 tablespoon soy sauce

3 cups mixed nuts (such as almonds, cashews, and pecans)

2 tablespoons wasabi powder (found at Asian stores and many supermarkets) or more to taste

3 tablespoons brown sugar

1/2 teaspoon freshly ground black pepper

2 teaspoons cornstarch

Preheat the oven to 275 degrees F. Line a rimmed baking sheet with greased foil or parchment paper. Whisk the egg white and soy sauce together until foamy. Add the nuts and toss to coat. Stir together the wasabi powder, sugar, pepper, and cornstarch in a large bowl. Add the nuts and toss to coat. Spread the nuts in a single layer on the prepared baking sheet and bake for 30 minutes. Reduce the temperature to 200 degrees F and continue baking for 20 minutes. Check often to ensure that the nuts are not burning, and rotate the pan as necessary. Let the nuts cool completely before serving.

NOTE: These nuts can be stored for up to a week in an airtight container.

Makes 3 cups

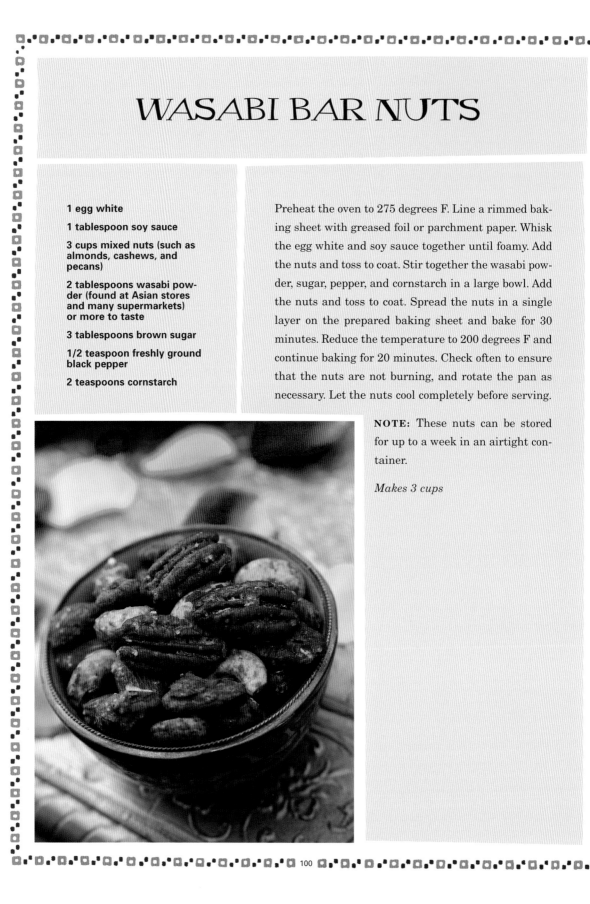

TANDOORI DRUMSTICKS

7 pounds chicken drumsticks
(about 30)

2 tablespoons finely
minced garlic

2 teaspoons finely
minced ginger

4 teaspoons paprika

1 1/2 tablespoons
ground cumin

1/2 teaspoon ground
red pepper

1/4 teaspoon ground
black pepper

1/4 teaspoon ground
cardamom

1/4 teaspoon ground cloves

2 teaspoons sugar

1 tablespoon fresh lemon juice

3 teaspoons salt

2 cups plain low-fat yogurt

Remove the skin from the drumsticks and use a knife to make deep diagonal slits 1 inch apart and halfway to the bone. In a large bowl, combine the garlic, ginger, paprika, cumin, red and black peppers, cardamom, cloves, sugar, lemon juice, salt, and yogurt. Add the chicken and toss, making sure the marinade seeps into each slit. Cover the bowl and leave in the refrigerator for up to 24 hours, stirring and turning the drumsticks at least once.

Preheat the oven to 450 degrees F. Lightly oil the rack of a broiler pan lined with foil. Using a slotted spoon, transfer the drumsticks to the oiled rack, reserving the rest of the marinade. Roast the chicken in the upper third of the oven for 15 minutes. Turn over the drumsticks and baste with the reserved marinade. Roast for another 15 to 20 minutes, or until the chicken is golden and cooked through. To brown the drumsticks more thoroughly, broil for the last few minutes.

Makes about 30 drumsticks

THAI SLAW

FOR THE DRESSING:

1/4 cup lime juice

1 tablespoon soy sauce

1 tablespoon minced ginger

2 teaspoons minced garlic

2 tablespoons honey

2 to 3 teaspoons Thai red curry paste

1 tablespoon sesame oil

1/2 cup peanut or canola oil

FOR THE SLAW:

7 cups finely sliced Napa cabbage

1 1/2 cups julienned carrots

1 large red or yellow pepper, thinly sliced

1 1/2 cups julienned snow peas

1/2 cup sliced scallions (green and white parts)

1/3 cup chopped cilantro

1/4 cup coarsely chopped roasted skinless peanuts

2 teaspoons salt

Put all the dressing ingredients in a glass jar and shake well. Toss the cabbage, carrots, pepper, snow peas, scallions, cilantro, and peanuts in a large bowl. Season with salt. Cover the mixture with the dressing and allow to marinate for 10 minutes before serving.

NOTE: This can be served in take-out containers and eaten with chopsticks.

Makes at least 12 servings

CANDY SUSHI

3 tablespoons unsalted butter

1 (10-ounce) bag large marshmallows (or 4 cups mini marshmallows)

6 cups Rice Krispies

12 (1/2-ounce) Fruit Roll-Ups (each about 4 by 4-inch square)

12 Twizzlers

Melt the butter in a saucepan over low heat. Add the marshmallows and stir until they melt. Add the Rice Krispies and stir to coat evenly. Spread about 1/2 cup of the Rice Krispies mixture evenly over one Fruit Roll-Up, leaving a 1-inch border along one side. Cut a Twizzler to the same length as the Fruit Roll-Up and press it in a horizontal line in the middle of the Rice Krispies mixture. Form a fat log (about 1 1/2 inches in diameter) by rolling the Fruit Roll-Up around the Rice Krispies mixture starting on the side without the border. Squeeze and compress the cereal mixture to form a neat log with as even and round dimensions as possible. Slice your "sushi" roll into 1/2-inch pieces with a wet serrated knife. Repeat with the remaining Fruit Roll-Ups, Rice Krispies mixture, and Twizzlers.

Makes about 90 pieces

CHAPTER NINE

HANDS-ON HALLOWEEN:

TRICKY TREATS

Halloween is a perennial event at Serendipity, as you are sure to find treats, costumes, and tricks on any day of the week. Many of our famous clients show up in unusual getups year-round. One spring day, Cher electrified the place in her pink leopard-print pants, boots, and cropped jacket. The next day she arrived wearing skintight jeans, a glittery tank top, and huge aviator glasses. On the afternoon that Cher ordered a "young chicken" sandwich, she was in full dominatrix mode, complete with black pants, black leather boots, and black leather jacket. For buying spooky gifts, she's a fan of our boutique where she can find items like a turquoise skull and wineglasses shaped like nuns.

If you can't convince Cher to come to your party, maybe you can have her pumpkin look-alike. Celebrated pumpkin artist Hugh McMahon likes to carve up the stars, but he's no serial killer. He sculpts them out of pumpkins. At Serendipity, he gave a pumpkin-carving demonstration, during which he turned pumpkins into Elizabeth Taylor, Bill Clinton, Cher, Marilyn Monroe, and Tom Cruise.

PARTY MENU

VEGETABLE CRUDITÉS
AND DIP

SWEET 'N' SEEDY CRUNCH
(page 111)

ROSEMARY'S BABY
BACK RIBS
(page 112)

MAKE-YOU-SHAKE
MOCHA CAKE
(page 114)

HOT MULLED WINE
(page 113)

PUMPKIN CARVING TIPS FROM HUGH McMAHON

1. Start with the right shape pumpkin. For a cat, choose a round shape, and so on. Check to see that the pumpkin has no rot spots and that it has a good stem.

2. Cut your main access hole from the bottom of the pumpkin, and remove the seeds and membranes. This will better preserve the pumpkin's shape.

3. Make a drawing of your design on paper first and then transfer your drawing to the pumpkin with a water-soluble marker.

4. To carve the pumpkin, use a thin paring knife and an Exacto knife. The paring knife works well for cutting out the broad, basic shapes. The Exacto is helpful for carving finer details and for removing just the thin outermost layer of pumpkin skin. Try to carve at varying depths, so that the shapes have more dimension and to allow different levels of light to shine through. A small electric lantern is better than a candle for illuminating the inside, since electric light lasts longer and shines more steadily.

5. Your carved pumpkin will last longer if you spray the cut edges with lemon juice and refrigerate it when it is not on display. And remember: The best carving tool is your imagination!

THE DEVIL'S MUSIC

1. "Halloween II," The Misfits
2. "This Is Halloween," The Citizens of Halloween
3. "Werewolf of London," Warren Zevon
4. "Straight to Hell," The Clash
5. "Witchy Woman," The Eagles
6. "Dark Hallow," Grateful Dead
7. "Sympathy for the Devil," The Rolling Stones
8. "Warlocks," Red Hot Chili Peppers
9. "Runnin' with the Devil," Van Halen
10. "Burning Hell," R.E.M.

CARDS THAT COME ALIVE

We took our inspiration for these glowing, Sleepy Hollow-esque invitations from McMahon's fabulous carved creations (see page 107). You'll find there's not much of a trick to it:

1. Find black note cards in stiff card stock, a sharp utility knife, colored tissue paper (red, orange, or yellow), and colored stationery.

2. On a plain white sheet of paper, draw the design for a spooky grimace, screeching cat, or grinning ghoul. With a utility knife, cut out the eyes, nose, mouth, and other details as desired from your template.

3. Unfold a black note card. Place your template over the front of the note card.

With the utility knife, follow the template to cut out the face of the note card.

4. On the inside of the card face, run a glue stick around the cutouts or dot with double-sided tape. Attach a sheet of red, orange, or yellow tissue paper, pressing lightly to keep the paper taut against the cutouts, and trim any overhang.

5. Print the information for your party onto brightly colored stationery cut to fit inside the card. Tear or very lightly singe the edges of the stationery before gluing it into the card. For added spookiness, stand each one in front of a small votive candle or tea light and watch them come to spine-tingling life.

WAITER, THERE'S A HAND IN MY PUNCH!

To make a ghoulish and gruesome punch bowl, start with a pair of thin latex gloves. In a pitcher or bowl with a pouring spout, combine 2 quarts of water with about 10 drops of red food coloring. Put on one glove and wash your hands while wearing it and rinse well. Remove the glove, turn it inside out, and fill it with the colored water. Tie off the bottom of the glove (to prevent leaking) and place it in the freezer at least 4 hours or until completely frozen. Repeat the process with the other glove. Once the gloves have frozen solid, cut or rip off the latex and remove the hand-shaped ice. Place the frozen hands in your punch bowl, and add your favorite punch (preferably a clear or light-colored drink to best set off the red hands).

HORROR HIGH ACTING SCHOOL

Many of our most celebrated clientele got their start in B-grade (or worse) horror movies. Rent these movies and try to spot the fledgling actors and actresses in their formative years. See if your friends can pick out the now-famous star or starlet. Present a DVD or poster of a horror movie from the list to the person who guesses the most right.

Carrie (John Travolta)
The Rocky Horror Picture Show (Susan Sarandon and Tim Curry)

Texas Chainsaw Massacre: The Next Generation (Renée Zellweger)
Amityville 3-D (Meg Ryan)
Tales from the Darkside: The Movie (Julianne Moore)
Nightmare on Elm Street (Johnny Depp)
Friday the 13th (Kevin Bacon)
The Fury (Daryl Hannah)
Return of the Killer Tomatoes (George Clooney)
The Keep (Ian McKellan)
Die! Die! My Darling! (Donald Sutherland)

FALLEN STARS: MAY THEY RISE AGAIN

This is a twist on the classic teenage slumber party game called Levitation. Ask for a volunteer to be the "fallen star" who lies flat on the floor with her arms crossed over her chest. The other participants (four to six others is best) surround her with one person at her head and one at her feet. These "levitators" sit on the floor either cross-legged or with their knees tucked under them and place two fingers of each hand under the fallen star. The person at the head is the leader, and he or she tells an anecdote about the star's death or a made-up story of how one of the characters the star was famous for playing met an untimely end. For example, you could describe how Holly Golightly accidentally choked on a diamond engagement ring hidden in her chocolate mousse, or how Norma Desmond tripped down the grand staircase in her house in *Sunset Boulevard*. Fill the story with dark humor. Upon finishing the tale, the leader starts to chant, "Light as a feather, stiff as a board," and everyone joins in. After several minutes of chanting, a signal is given, and with almost no effort, the star rises once more—but don't let her come crashing to earth again.

HANDBAGS TO DIE FOR

Divide the number of guests you expect at your party in half and buy that many pairs of black stretchy gloves. These can be purchased at running stores, flea markets, and various clothing stores. Buy the largest size available.

Decorate the gloves with painted press-on nails in orange, red, or other bright color; or glue a spider ring or other plastic Halloween ring on one of the fingers.

To create a handle for the bag, use strong fabric glue to attach a length of creepy-colored ribbon (10 inches or longer, depending on your fashion preference).

Glue a strip of marabou or feather boa around the cuff of each glove.

Stuff the bags with candy, so it fills out like a hand, and then give each guest a hand.

SWEET'N'SEEDY CRUNCH

2 cups pumpkin seeds

2 tablespoons vegetable oil or olive oil

1 teaspoon salt

1 cup dried cranberries

1/2 cup golden raisins

1 cup Chex breakfast cereal

1 cup popped popcorn

1/2 cup sunflower seeds

1 cup pretzel sticks

If you are working with seeds that you have just removed from a pumpkin, preheat the oven to 275 degrees F. Rinse the seeds well in cold water and pat dry, discarding the stringy membranes. Transfer the seeds to a large bowl and mix in the oil and salt, stirring well to coat. Spread the seeds in a single layer on a baking sheet lined with greased foil or parchment paper. Bake the seeds for 12 to 15 minutes, or until they turn crisp and golden.

When the pumpkin seeds have cooled, pour them into a large mixing bowl. Add the cranberries, raisins, cereal, popcorn, sunflower seeds, and pretzel sticks and mix well.

Makes 6 cups

ROSEMARY'S BABY BACK RIBS

4 pounds baby back pork ribs

Salt and coarsely ground pepper

1 1/2 tablespoons vegetable oil

1/2 cup minced onion

1 cup tomato paste

1/2 cup distilled white vinegar

3/4 cup brown sugar

1/2 cup molasses

1 tablespoon Worcestershire sauce

2 tablespoons chili powder

1 teaspoon garlic powder

2 teaspoons dry mustard

1/4 teaspoon cayenne pepper

1/2 ounce bitter chocolate, grated

Preheat the oven to 300 degrees F. Cut each full rack of ribs in half. Sprinkle with salt and pepper. Wrap each half rack in foil and bake for 2 1/2 hours.

Heat the oil in a large saucepan over medium heat. Cook the onion for 5 minutes, or until softened. Stir in 2 cups of water, the tomato paste, vinegar, brown sugar, molasses, Worcestershire sauce, 2 teaspoons salt, chili powder, garlic powder, mustard, cayenne, and chocolate. Bring the mixture to a boil and reduce the heat. Simmer for 1 1/4 hours, uncovered, or until the sauce thickens. Remove the saucepan from the heat.

Preheat an outdoor grill to high. Remove the ribs from the oven and let stand for 10 minutes. Remove the racks from the foil and place on the grill. Grill for 3 to 4 minutes on each side. Brush the ribs with the

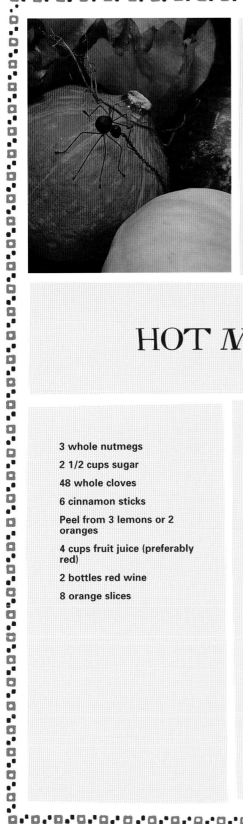

barbecue sauce while they're grilling and again just prior to serving them.

NOTE: If no grill is available, finish the ribs in an oven preheated to 450 degrees F. Brush the ribs with barbecue sauce and cook for approximately 20 minutes.

VARIATION: For a simpler version, substitute prepared barbecue sauce for homemade.

Makes 6 to 8 servings

HOT MULLED WINE

3 whole nutmegs

2 1/2 cups sugar

48 whole cloves

6 cinnamon sticks

Peel from 3 lemons or 2 oranges

4 cups fruit juice (preferably red)

2 bottles red wine

8 orange slices

Crush the nutmegs with a nutcracker or a mallet. Pour 1 1/4 cups of water into a large saucepan. Add the sugar, cloves, nutmeg, cinnamon, and citrus peel. Bring to a boil and cook for several minutes. Strain the hot liquid and discard the solids. Stir the fruit juice and wine into the strained liquid. Float the orange slices on top and serve hot.

Makes about 3 quarts

MAKE-YOU-SHAKE MOCHA CAKE

1 pound (4 sticks) unsalted butter

4 cups brown sugar

4 eggs

3 teaspoons vanilla extract

10 ounces unsweetened chocolate, melted and cooled

2 3/4 cups unsifted cake flour

1/2 teaspoon salt

1 teaspoon baking soda

1 cup sour cream

4 tablespoons instant espresso

1 1/2 cups lukewarm water

Preheat the oven to 350 degrees F.

In the bowl of an electric mixer, cream the butter and brown sugar until light and fluffy. Beat in the eggs until the mixture is creamy. Add the vanilla and beat in the chocolate.

In a small bowl, stir together the flour, salt, and baking soda. Add the flour mixture to the liquid mixture, alternating with the sour cream. Add the flour and sour cream in three parts, making sure to scrape down the sides of the bowl following each addition. Dissolve the espresso in the lukewarm water. Slowly stir the dissolved espresso into the batter.

Use parchment paper to line two 10-inch cake pans. Greased and flour the parchment paper liners. Divide the batter into the two pans. Bake for about 60 minutes, or until a knife inserted in the center of the cake comes out clean and the top springs back when touched lightly. Remove the cake pans from the oven and let them cool for 20 minutes. Carefully remove the cake layers from the pans and let them cool completely on a wire rack. Using a serrated knife, divide each cake into two layers. Frost the layers with Cobweb Icing (page 115).

Makes 4 (10-inch) layers

COBWEB ICING

6 egg whites

7 1/2 to 9 cups confectioners' sugar

3 teaspoons vanilla extract

1/4 cup freshly squeezed orange juice

Black or dark brown food coloring (brown can be made by an equal amount of red, blue, and yellow food coloring)

Place the egg whites in a large bowl. Using an electric mixer, beat the whites on high speed until soft peaks form. Add the confectioners' sugar, vanilla, and orange juice, and continue beating until the mixture is thick and shiny. The consistency of the icing should make it easy to spread. If it seems too thick, add more orange juice; if it's too thin, add more confectioners' sugar.

Set aside one-fourth of the white icing to make the cobweb design on top of the cake. Using the rest of the white icing, frost in between the layers and on the sides and top of the cake. To the reserved icing, add black or dark brown food coloring until it looks quite dark. Spoon the dark icing into a pastry bag with a tip or into a plastic squeeze bottle. Starting at the center of the cake, pipe a spiral of dark icing from the center to the outer edge of the cake. Drag a sharp knife point from the center of the spiral out to the edge of the cake. Wipe the knife clean, move about an inch to the right or left, and drag the knife in the opposite direction from the outer edge to the middle of the cake. Continue until you have worked your way around the cake to form a cobweb.

NOTE: You can add to the cake's decoration with spiders made from chocolate chip bodies and black licorice legs.

Makes 8 cups (enough to frost one 4 (10-inch)-layer cake)

CHAPTER 10

KICKING UP YOUR HOLIDAY HEELS:

HOMEMADE SPARKLE

To relieve end-of-the-year stress, we like to kick up our heels with our friends the Rockettes, Radio City Music Hall's world-famous dancers. They've even got their own "mocktail" named after them at Serendipity: the Christmas Spectacular Frrrozen White Chocolate. Instead of a tree one season, we featured a Rockette window, where a life-size Rockette mannequin shared the stage with a giant Frrrozen White Chocolate set against a green velvet backdrop.

You may not be able to pull off a Rockette window in your home, but you can surely make space for some high-kicking times. Convert one room to a "ballroom" by clearing out all the furniture from the center. Fill the room with as many gold and silver helium-filled balloons tied with silver strings as possible. Rent a disco ball from a party store and attach it to an overhead fixture in the middle of the room, or find miniature disco balls and hang them from various spots on the ceiling, in doorways, or along the mantelpiece.

For music, keep it simple. Hire a DJ or load up your iPod with a long playlist. We were lucky enough to have Paula Abdul and five of her friends come to the restaurant for ice cream sundaes on New Year's Day. A party of four spontaneously auditioned for her, accompanied by music that was playing on our sound system.

When it comes to holiday decor, it's easy to get overwhelmed, but again, make it simple. Lots of pine boughs and pretty twigs are an inexpensive way to add natural charm and a woodsy scent to your home. And when was the last time you made cranberry and popcorn garlands? Don't forget to hang mistletoe tied with red and green ribbons in every doorway for stolen kisses. Buy small poinsettias for the table. Mix and match red and green china in different patterns for Christmas or black and white for New Year's.

Party Menu

SELECTION OF FINE CHEESES

FILET MIGNON WITH CREAMED
SPINACH ON GARLIC TOAST
(page 124)

LUCKY NEW YEAR DIP
(page 125)

COCONUT-CUPPED AMBROSIA
(page 123)

MAZEL TOV MATZOH TOFFEE
(page 126)

CHAMPAGNE SNOWBALLS
(page 127)

BAUBLES IN THE MAIL

For a fun invite that does double duty, make decorative baubles from paper. Buy heavy card stock paper in holiday colors and some square envelopes to match. Cut the paper into circles about four inches in diameter (make sure your circles will fit inside the envelopes). Use stencils (or your best handwriting) to put festive sayings on one or both sides of the cards. With a hole puncher, create a hole at the top. String yarn through this and tie into a knot. This way guests can hang their invites up as reminders and as easy decorations—whether for the tree or anywhere around the house.

CLASSIC AND NOT-SO CLASSIC CAROLS

1. "Jingle Bell Rock," Bobby Helms
2. "Santa's Messin' with the Kid," Lynyrd Skynyrd
3. "I Saw Mommy Kissing Santa Claus," Jackson 5
4. "White Christmas," Bing Crosby
5. "Santa Baby," Madonna
6. "This Is the New Year," Death Cab for Cutie
7. "Thank God It's Christmas," Queen
8. "Rockin' Around the Christmas Tree," Brenda Lee
9. "Santa Claus Is Back in Town," Elvis Presley
10. "Silent Night," Stevie Nicks
11. "Have Yourself a Merry Little Christmas," Judy Garland
12. "The Ghost of Christmas Past," Stephen Warbeck
13. "Happy New Year," Abba
14. "All I Want for Christmas Is You," Mariah Carey

NO SNOW? MAKE A SNOW GLOBE!

1. Choose a clear glass jar for your snow globe. A variety of common jars, such as baby food, jelly, or olive jars, work well. Pick the prettiest jar you can find and make sure to remove all the labels and make it spotlessly clean.

2. With serendipity as your guiding star, design your snow globe scene by picking an unusual holiday ornament, a porcelain figurine, small plastic toys, seashells, game pieces from old Monopoly sets, part of an old key chain, tourist mementos like a miniature Eiffel Tower, or dollhouse items—anything that will remain intact while wet. Make sure that your scene will fit within the diameter of the jar.

3. Before you glue your scene to the jar's lid, make sure that it will all be visible once the jar is closed, as some jars have deeper lids than others. If it is difficult to see, elevate the scene by gluing it to a small plastic bottle lid to create a base. Glue the scene to the base and then place the base in the center of the inside of the lid. Secure your scene to the inside of the jar's lid (or to the base) using a glue gun, silicone, or aquarium sealant (available at craft or hardware stores). Allow this assembly to dry and set according to the glue manufacturer's instructions.

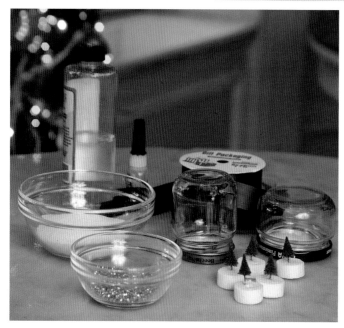

4. Use another small jar to test the snow fall. Fill the test jar with distilled water combined with either a few drops of glycerin, mineral oil, or baby oil. Add a scant teaspoon of glitter and shake it to test the effect. If the "snow" looks too sparse, add more glitter. If you have no glitter, you can also make snow by crushing eggshells inside a heavy-duty plastic bag with a rolling pin. Test whatever material you select in the same way as the glitter. Be creative: Add bits of costume jewelry or food coloring to the liquid and make a brand-new kind of snow.

5. Working over a sink, fill the real jar with the distilled water and oil or glycerin combination and add the glitter or other snowlike material. Fill the jar to the very top with liquid. Invert the ornament assembly into the water and screw the lid firmly in place. Some liquid will be displaced and spill over the top of the jar. Wipe the jar dry and shake it for a test run.

6. Decorate the top of the lid with pretty fabric and ribbon, if you wish.

7. Shake, shake, shake, and let it snow!

A CHORUS LINE OF COOKIES

For a low-key party before the holidays get into full swing, throw a potluck cookie and candy exchange. Invite guests to come in their favorite pair of jeans. Each person brings about three dozen homemade cookies or candies, which are exchanged at the end of the evening. Encourage guests to make cookies in whimsical shapes, painted with bright-colored icing, or blinged up with silver balls or gold-covered Jordan almonds. Another idea is to bake cookie ornaments by creating a small hole in the dough with a drinking straw before baking. Carefully remove the small dot of dough if it does not come out when you lift up the straw. After the cookies are baked and cool, simply thread a wire or ribbon through the hole for hanging the ornament. As guests arrive with their sweets, remove them from the containers or tins, display them on your festive table, and each guest refills his or her tin with a new assortment of cookies and candies to bring home.

MAMA TOLD ME YOU BETTER SWAP AROUND

Serendipity's boutique has carried everything from one-color jigsaw puzzles to chocolate foot cream to love potions. We delight in such amusing and frivolous gifts, and this is the perfect game to play when exchanging them. It is also known as the White Elephant Game because in Burmese culture, an albino elephant is rare and must be well cared for despite the financial burden to its owner. Have fun while you unload some quirky holiday presents at the same time.

✳ Guests bring a wrapped present they have received recently but know they will never use—for example, a brass belt buckle in the shape of an oil rig. Participants can also buy an inexpensive gag present, but each present must be wrapped.

✳ Every player picks a number from a hat which has as many numbers as players (i.e., 1 through 20 if there are 20 players).

✳ The player who has drawn No. 1 starts the game by choosing any wrapped present and opening it in front of the group.

✳ The next player may either steal the first player's gift or choose another unopened gift.

✳ The subsequent players choose to either steal a gift from those who had a lower number or to pick from the remaining wrapped gifts.

✳ If your gift is stolen, you immediately get to replace it by stealing any other unwrapped gift or by unwrapping a new gift. Hopefully, whoever has the best sense of humor will end up with the green-and-red velvet jingle-bell thong!

COCONUT-CUPPED AMBROSIA

4 egg whites

1 1/4 cups sugar

4 cups dried unsweetened coconut

6 navel oranges

1 ruby red grapefruit

1 cup diced fresh pineapple

1 cup sour cream

2 cups shredded sweetened coconut

2 cups mini marshmallows

Fresh mint

Preheat the oven to 350 degrees F. Combine the egg whites, 1 cup of sugar, and the unsweetened coconut in a large mixing bowl. With a spoon or damp hands, press the mixture into a mini-muffin tin, covering the base and sides to make a shell. Bake for 10 to 12 minutes, or until golden. Cool for 1 minute before carefully removing the shells to a wire rack.

Peel the oranges and grapefruit to remove all the membrane and white pith. Cut the fruit into small pieces. In a medium bowl, combine the orange, grapefruit, and pineapple with the remaining 1/4 cup of sugar. Let the mixture sit until the sugar dissolves. Add the sour cream, sweetened coconut, and mini marshmallows, gently stirring to combine, and chill. When ready to serve, scoop the mixture into the cooled coconut shells. Garnish each shell with a sprig of mint, if desired.

Makes 16 cups or 32 mini-cups

FILET MIGNON WITH CREAMED SPINACH ON GARLIC TOAST

3 pounds baby spinach

1 1/4 cups whole milk

1 cup heavy cream

1 small onion, finely chopped

8 tablespoons (1 stick) unsalted butter

1/4 cup all-purpose flour

1/8 teaspoon freshly grated nutmeg

Salt and pepper

1 loaf French bread, sliced into 1/3-inch-thick rounds

2 teaspoons minced garlic

2 pounds filet mignon, cooked medium-rare, sliced into 1/4-inch-thick rounds

To make the creamed spinach, cook the spinach in 1 inch of boiling salted water, stirring constantly, until wilted, 1 to 2 minutes. Cook in batches if necessary. Drain in a colander and rinse under cold running water until cool. Squeeze small handfuls of the spinach to extract as much moisture as possible, then coarsely chop.

Heat the milk and cream in a small saucepan over moderate heat, stirring, until warm. Cook the onion in 4 tablespoons of the butter in a 3-quart heavy saucepan over moderately low heat until softened, about 4 minutes. Whisk in the flour. Continue whisking for 3 minutes, or until a thick roux forms. Add the warm milk mixture in a fast stream, whisking constantly to prevent lumps, and cook, whisking until thickened, for 3 to 4 minutes. Stir in the nutmeg, chopped spinach, and salt and pepper to taste, and cook until heated through.

To make the garlic toasts, place the rounds of bread in a single layer on a baking sheet. Melt the remaining 4 tablespoons of butter. Combine the garlic with the melted butter in a small bowl. Brush the tops of each bread round with garlic butter. Broil the bread in the oven for a couple of minutes, watching carefully that it does not burn. Remove from the oven to cool.

When the toast is cool enough to handle, arrange the rounds on a serving platter. Place a tablespoon of creamed spinach on each piece of toast topped off by a slice of filet mignon.

NOTE: To save time, use prepared creamed spinach instead of homemade.

Makes 32 appetizers, 6 to 8 servings

LUCKY NEW YEAR DIP

2 tablespoons unsalted butter

1/2 cup chopped onion

1 garlic clove, finely minced

2 1/2 cups shredded sharp Cheddar cheese

2 (15-ounce) cans black-eyed peas, drained and rinsed

1 jalapeño pepper, seeds removed, finely chopped

Salt and pepper

Melt the butter in a medium saucepan over medium-low heat. Add the chopped onion and sauté until golden. Add the garlic and cook for 30 seconds longer. Turn the heat to low and add the cheese, stirring until melted. Add the black-eyed peas and chopped jalapeño. Cook for 5 minutes, stirring constantly. Add salt and pepper to taste. Serve hot in a slow cooker or chafing dish with chips, crackers, or crudités for dipping.

Makes about 4 cups

MAZEL TOV MATZOH TOFFEE

4 to 6 unsalted matzohs

16 tablespoons (2 sticks) unsalted butter

1 cup firmly packed brown sugar

3/4 to 1 cup white and dark chocolate chips or coarsely chopped semisweet chocolate

Preheat the oven to 375 degrees F. Line a rimmed cookie sheet with foil. Cover the foil with parchment paper. Arrange the matzohs on the bottom of the cookie sheet in an even layer, breaking extra pieces as required to fill in the space.

In a 3-quart, heavy-bottomed saucepan, combine the butter and the brown sugar. Cook over medium heat, stirring constantly, until the mixture comes to a boil, about 2 to 4 minutes. Boil for 3 minutes, stirring constantly. Remove from the heat and pour the caramel over the matzohs, covering them completely. Place the baking sheet in the oven and immediately reduce the heat to 350 degrees F. Bake for 15 minutes, checking every few minutes to make sure the mixture is not burning. Remove the cookie sheet from the oven and immediately sprinkle the chips or chopped chocolate over the hot mixture. Let stand for 5 minutes, allowing the chocolate to melt before spreading it over the matzohs. While still warm, break the matzohs into squares or irregular shapes. Chill the pieces in the freezer, still resting on the cookie sheets, about 2 hours or until set.

Note: For a delectable homemade gift or party favor, put a handful of matzohs in decorative cellophane bags with colorful ties. These can be stored in the refrigerator, freezer, or at room temperature.

Makes about 1 1/2 pounds toffee

CHAMPAGNE SNOWBALLS

2 cups lemon or lime sherbet

1/2 cup Champagne or sparkling wine

Ice cubes

Puree the sherbet, Champagne or sparkling wine, and ice in a blender. Pour into a glass and serve immediately.

Makes 1 serving

First published in the United States of America in 2008
by Universe Publishing, A Division of
Rizzoli International Publications, Inc.
300 Park Avenue South
New York, NY 10010
www.rizzoliusa.com

Project Editor: Joseph Calderone
Project Assistant: Joann Lee
Designers: Paul Kepple, Susan Van Horn, Headcase Design
Publisher: Charles Miers, Universe Publishing
Editor: Christopher Steighner, Universe Publishing
Craft Stylist: Jonathan Jarrett
Food Stylist: Rebecca Fisher
Pumpkin and Melon Carver: Hugh McMahon

2008 2009 2010 2011 / 10 9 8 7 6 5 4 3 2 1

Distributed in the U.S. trade by Random House, New York

Printed in China

ISBN-10: 0-7893-1694-3
ISBN-13: 978-0-7893-1694-3

Library of Congress Catalog Control Number: 2007909706